S0-BOC-460

The Unmarried Father

THE UNMARRIED FATHER

New Approaches For Helping Unmarried Young Parents

Reuben Pannor
Fred Massarik
Byron Evans

Springer Publishing Co., Inc., New York

SPRINGER PUBLISHING COMPANY, INC.
200 Park Avenue South, New York, New York

Acknowledgments

We wish to express our appreciation to the Board of Directors of Vista Del Mar Child-Care Service and the Research Service Bureau of the Jewish Federation – Council of Greater Los Angeles for their support and commitment to the study of unmarried fathers and unmarried mothers upon which this book is based.

We are indebted to the Children's Bureau, U. S. Department of Health, Education and Welfare for the award of a three-year grant (Demonstration Grant D-128) in June 1963, without which the initial study would not have been possible.

The study provided an opportunity for joint cooperation between research staff, social work practitioners, and volunteers. We wish to express our thanks and appreciation to the following social workers, who were an integral part of the study team: Matille Rowan, Rosalyn Benitez, Murray Klickstein, Ruth Drucker, and Robert Rufrano; to David Shichor, Research Assistant; and to Faye Nisenbaum, Jodee Rossi, and Rebecca Schulman, for their invaluable assistance in the technical aspects of the study.

Finally, we are indebted to the 96 unmarried fathers and 222 unmarried mothers who participated in this study with the hope that it would be of help to others.

THE AUTHORS

Library of Congress Catalog Card Number: 77-130683
Standard Book Number: 8261-1171-8

PRINTED IN U.S.A.

Contents

	Introduction	1
	The Unmarried Father: From Shadow to Reality. Part I	4
I	Illegitimacy as a Social Problem	11
II	The Study Plan	21
III	Some Basic Facts	32
IV	The Unmarried Father – Reachable	44
V	Sexual Ideology and the Sexual Act	64
	The Unmarried Father: From Shadow to Reality. Part II	75
VI	Making the Decision: The Fate of the Child	84
VII	Background and Personality of Unwed Parents	97
VIII	The Parents	123
IX	The Role of the Social Worker	135
X	Prevention	147
	The Unmarried Father: From Shadow to Reality. Part III	157
	Appendix	161
	Author Index	190
	Subject Index	191

Tables

1. Projection of Success in Reaching Unmarried Fathers and Actual Experience in Reaching Them 24
2. Ages of Unmarried Mothers in the Study and in the United States 32
3. Ages of Unmarried Mothers and Unmarried Fathers in the Study and in the State of California 33
4. Age Differentials of Unmarried "Couples" in the Study 35
5. Social Class of Unmarried Parents in the Study (Utilizing Hollingshead's Formula) 36
6. Education of Unmarried Parents in the Study Group 37
7. Unmarried Mothers' Marital Status at Time Agency Was Contacted 38
8. Marital Status of Unmarried Mother – Unmarried Father Partnerships, Vista Del Mar Study 40
9. Unmarried Fathers' Marital Status at Time Agency Was First Contacted 41
9-A. Comparative Marital Status of Unmarried Mothers and Unmarried Fathers at Time Agency Was First Contacted 41
10. Percentages of Unmarried Parents Who Were Adopted Children 42
11. Incidence of Out-of-Wedlock Pregnancy for 79 Unmarried Couples 43
12. Percentages of Unmarried Mothers Who Agreed and Who Did Not Agree to Unmarried Father's Involvement with the Agency (Eliminating Control Where Involvement Was Not Sought) 50
13. Relationship Between Unmarried Mother's Agreement to Father's Involvement and Success in Reaching Unmarried Fathers 51

14. Extent to Which Local and Non-Local Unmarried Mothers Participated Actively in Involving the Unmarried Fathers with the Agency 53
15. Relationship Between Unmarried Mother's Active Assistance in Effecting Unmarried Father's Involvement and Agency's Success in Reaching the Unmarried Father 53
16. Extent to Which Male Worker Used Particular Motivational Appeals to Bring About the Unmarried Father's Involvement, by Age Category 58
17. Unmarried Parents' Interviews with Agency Caseworkers 59
18. Projection of Success and Actual Success in Reaching Unmarried Fathers 60
19. Percentages of Unmarried Fathers Living in the Community Who Were Seen and Were Not Seen (Experimental and Control Exception) 61
20. Extent to Which Unmarried Parents Viewed Sex as "Fun" 65
21. Guilt Feelings of Unmarried Parents as Perceived by Caseworkers 66
22. Meanings Unmarried Parents Associate with the Sex Act 68, 69
23. Extent to Which Unmarried Parents Regarded Pregnancy as Something That "Just Happened," as Perceived by Workers 71
24. Extent to Which Unmarried Parents Knew About Contraceptives 72
25. Extent to Which Unmarried Mothers and Unmarried Fathers Felt That Obtaining Contraceptives Was a Problem 72
26. Extent to Which the Goal of Helping the Unmarried Mother Make the Appropriate Decision with Respect to the Baby's Future Was Reached for Experimental and Control Groups 87
27. Extent to Which Unmarried Mothers Kept Their Babies as Compared with Expressed Desire to Keep Early in Casework—Father Seen 88
28. Extent to Which Unmarried Mothers Kept Their Babies as Compared with Expressed Desire to Keep Early in Casework—Father Not Seen 88

29. Actions Taken by Unmarried Mothers in Respect to Their Out-of-Wedlock Children 89
30. Mothers Who Kept, by Category of Married/Did Not Marry, and Unmarried Father Seen/Not Seen 90
31. Extent to Which Unmarried Fathers Approved of Unmarried Mother's Final Decision Concerning Plans for the Baby, by Category of Fathers Seen and Not Seen 91
32. Frequency with Which Male Caseworkers Raised the Issue of Financial Contribution by the Father 94
33. Extent of Solicitation and Persons Solicited for Help in Expressing to Unmarried Fathers the Importance of Their Financial Participation 95
34. Religion of Unmarried Mothers and Unmarried Fathers in the Study, by Partnership 99
35. Comparison of Vista Del Mar Unmarried Mothers 18 and Under with Those 19 and Over, on Jewish Identity Test 100
36. Frequency of Personal Disjunctions for Unmarried Parents in the Study, Expressed in Percentages 112
37. Comparison of Mean Number of Disjunctions for Jessor's Group of Male Anglo-Saxon Non-Deviants and Vista Del Mar's Group of Unmarried Fathers 113
38. Comparison of Mean Number of Disjunctions for Jessor's Group of Female Anglo-Saxon Non-Deviants and Vista Del Mar's Group of Unmarried Mothers 113
39. Alienation Scores for Vista Del Mar Unmarried Mothers and Female Anglo-Saxon Non-Deviants 114
40. Alienation Scores for Vista Del Mar Unmarried Fathers and Male Anglo-Saxon Non-Deviants 115
41. Attitude Toward Deviance – Jessor's Group of Anglo Male Non-Deviants and Vista Del Mar's Group of Unmarried Fathers 115
42. Attitude Toward Deviance – Jessor's Group of Anglo Female Non-Deviants and Vista Del Mar's Group of Unmarried Mothers 116
43. Degree of Perceived Conflict Between Parents of Unmarried Parents 117
44. Frequency of Caseworkers' Assessment that Engaging in Sexual Relationship Proved Masculinity/Femininity to Unmarried Parents 118

45. Family Constellations of Parents of Unmarried Parents in the Study 126
46. Unmarried Parents' Assessment of Their Parents' Marriages in Vista Del Mar Study 127
47. Focus of Decision-Making in Parental Unit 128
48. Dominant Member of Parental Unit as Perceived by Unmarried Parents 128
49. Degree of Perceived Conflict Between Parents of Unmarried Parents 129
50. Frequency with Which Unmarried Mothers in the Study and Their Parents Attended Church/Synagogue 130
51. Frequency with Which Unmarried Fathers in the Study and Their Parents Attended Church/Synagogue 130
52. Extent to Which Parents of Unmarried Mothers (Under 18) Were Critical of Self Concerning Role in Relation to Daughter 131
53. Extent to Which Parents of Unmarried Fathers (Under 21) Were Critical of Self Concerning Role in Relation to Son 131
54. Extent to Which Parents of Unmarried Mothers Were Concerned about What Others Would Think of Them as Parents 132
55. Extent to Which Parents of Unmarried Fathers Were Concerned about What Others Would Think of Them as Parents 133
56. Extent to Which Parents of Unmarried Mothers Were Concerned about What Others Would Think of Their Pregnant Daughter 133
57. Extent to Which Parents of Unmarried Fathers Were Concerned about What Others Would Think of Their Son 134
58. Extent to Which Various Motivational Factors Contributed Toward Unmarried Fathers Keeping Agency Appointments, by Age Category (Caseworkers' Assessments) 141

Figures

Figure 1. Relationship of Numbers of Unmarried Fathers Reached to Agreement and Assistance of Unmarried Mothers 52
Figure 2. Distribution of Frequency with which Unmarried Mothers Aided in Reaching Unmarried Fathers and Success in Reaching Unmarried Father by Residence (Local and Non-Local) 54
Figure 3. Distribution of Contributions Made by Unmarried Fathers to Vista Del Mar for Meeting Maternity Costs Incurred by Unmarried Mothers 96
Figure 4. Profile Sheet for the California Psychological Inventory: Male 104
Figure 5. Profile Sheet for the California Psychological Inventory: Female 105
Figure 6. Preventive Factors that Might Have Mitigated Against Out-of-Wedlock Pregnancy for Unmarried Fathers and Unmarried Mothers, as Seen by Caseworkers 148

Preface

Social workers at Vista Del Mar Child-Care Service in Los Angeles, after working with unmarried mothers over a period of years, arrived at the conclusion that the phenomenon of illegitimacy and its attending problems were closely allied to the unmarried father and his relationship to the unmarried mother.

We also recognized that systematic research in this area was long overdue. With the support of a grant from the United States Children's Bureau, we began a comprehensive study that focused on the unmarried father and his impact upon the unmarried mother and the decision-making about the baby. This book contains the findings of that research.

Although this book deals with the unmarried father and efforts to help him to act in a more responsible way towards the unmarried mother and the child, it is not enough to say to a young father, "Be responsible." While the young mother can often assume her role as wife and mother with relative ease, the teenage father is much less frequently prepared for the responsibilities of being a husband and father. We must provide him with help so that becoming responsible can, indeed, be an attainable objective. Comprehensive services, which should include educational help, vocational training, help in obtaining employment, economic assistance, help in finding adequate housing, marriage counseling, and family life and sex education, are needed to meet this challenge.

In neglecting the families created by teenage parents,

America is neglecting an important segment of its population. The United States Children's Bureau estimates that 600,000 girls under 20 years of age gave birth to babies in 1970. Most of these babies were born to teenage parents who were married, and a large number were born to those who got married after the mother conceived. But thousands of young girls had their babies out of wedlock. Many, including an increasing number of middle-class Caucasian girls, chose to keep their babies outside of marriage, although a good number of these girls will marry at some future time. (For others, liberalized abortion laws and changing attitudes towards abortion, will make it possible to terminate unwanted pregnancies).

The parents of these new families are scarcely more than children themselves, thrust into the role of raising children. When illegitimate births complicate the problem, their chances of succeeding in the parental role diminish. Unfortunately, little help has been given to these young people; they have been left on their own to succeed or fail. We have lacked the perception to see the strengths they possess, or to see that they and their children can become important assets to our country. It is, therefore, necessary for us to have a better understanding of this phenomenon and to make available the kind of help that will strengthen and stabilize their families. In doing this, we must give special attention to helping the young father properly assume his role.

In helping young parents to reshape their lives and to provide more adequately for their babies, we are strengthening the next generation, and the next, and still the next.

October, 1970 REUBEN PANNOR
Los Angeles

Introduction

Most of the reports that have been written on the subject of unmarried parenthood have dealth with the unmarried mother. Little indeed has been said about the other protagonist in the drama of illegitimacy—the father of the child born out of wedlock.

The reasons for this omission are many and complex. In western culture, the male is often regarded as a relatively free agent whose premarital or extramarital indiscretions are, in some measure, tacitly accepted or overlooked. To say that unmarried fatherhood has been openly condoned may be an overstatement, yet it is not without its kernel of truth. We still place the major onus for out-of-wedlock conception on the girl. The boy is often subject only to raised eyebrows, if that, along with considerable *sub rosa* approval of this proof of his masculinity.

Whenever social constraints *have* been placed on the man, they have been directed, sometimes with an undertone of vindictiveness for his alleged wrongdoings, toward one of two objectives: 1) "Do right by the girl—marry her," as though marriage were necessarily the ideal answer, magically wiping away all problems of mother, father, and child. The psychology of the "shotgun" wedding still survives, particularly in the minds of the older generation. 2) "All right, so don't marry the girl—but *pay* for your misdeeds." This view demands financial support, particularly for expenses connected with the child's birth.

Neither of these solutions takes into consideration the genuine complexity of the past, present, and future of all the parties concerned, or the network of relationships—healthy and deficient—that is connected with the act of conceiving a child out of wedlock. So far, this tangle of relationships has been almost entirely ignored. The mother is the person who has stood out in bold relief—subject to pity, scorn, mysterious disappearance, even casual acceptance and, in some measure, to professional care and mature attention. Only in recent years has our vista broadened and progress been made in facing the totality of the situation and the multitude of problems that inevitably occur in what has been oversimplified as "unmarried motherhood." In this book we shall bring to light some of the facts regarding the effects of out-of-wedlock parenthood on the other actor in this age-old drama—the unmarried father.

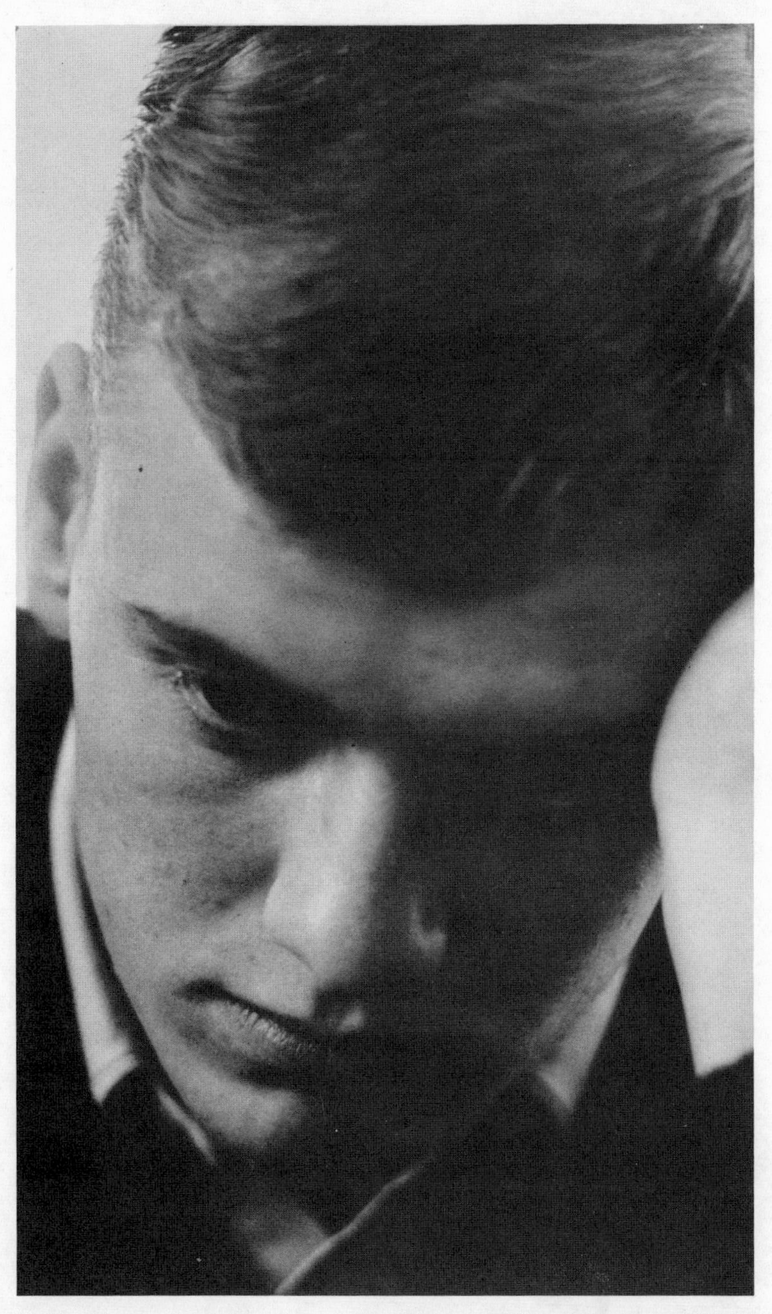

Black Star, Werner Wolff

The Unmarried Father: From Shadow to Reality: Part I

Don lay sprawled across his bed, his lanky 17-year-old body contorted into one of the typical adolescent postures that so annoyed his mother. His math book lay open beside him, but he wasn't really studying. He couldn't concentrate. His two-year-old brother in the room across the hall was singing to himself in his crib, and next to Don's room, his seven-year-old sister was carrying on an animated conversation with her dolls. But it wasn't his brother and sister that kept him from studying. He just couldn't seem to concentrate on his schoolwork lately. The telephone rang, but before he could untangle his arms and legs to answer it, his mother answered it on the downstairs extension. "Telephone! It's Betty!" His sister next door began to sing:

> *"Don and Betty sitting in a tree*
> *K-I-S-S-I-N-G.*
> *First comes love, then comes marriage,*
> *Then comes. . . ."*

Don closed the door to his room with a kick, picked up the receiver, waited for the click that meant his mother had replaced the receiver downstairs, and said, "Hi, Bets."

"Don? Are you alone? Can you talk?"

Don hardly recognized the tremulous voice at the other end of the line. "Yeah, Hon. I'm alone. What's the matter?"

"Don, it's what we were afraid of. Oh, Don, I'm pregnant."

Don sat down slowly on his bed. He opened his mouth to speak, but he couldn't make any words come out. He felt just like he had once when a hard-thrown forward pass had hit him in the stomach and knocked him to his knees.

"Don? Are you there?"

The desperation in the girl's voice reached him, and he managed to blurt out, "Yeah, I'm here. Bets, are you sure?"

"I'm sure," she whispered.

Don let out a long, slow breath. He felt sick, his palms were wet, and the receiver felt heavy and slippery in his hand. "Listen, Betty, I—I've got to think. Have you—have you told your parents?"

"No, how can I?" The girl began to cry softly, and he knew he couldn't listen any longer.

"I'll call you back, Bets. I've got to think. Don't—look, don't cry. I'll call you back."

"Okay," she whispered.

He put down the receiver heavily, and buried his face in his hands. Oh, how had this happened? That was a stupid thought; he knew perfectly well how *it had happened, but* why? *He and Betty hadn't wanted to make a baby; they'd just wanted to try making love. How could a baby—a* baby*—have come out of it? He felt panic well up within him, and he knew if he didn't move, get up, walk around, he was going to be sick. He pulled on a sweater, ran out of his room, down the stairs, and out the front door.*

"Don? Don!" His mother came to the door and called after him, but he didn't answer her, didn't even look back, just kept on running, blindly, until he was out of breath and couldn't run any more. Then he slowed to a walk, and tried to think. Think about Betty, he told himself, and what she must be going through. How could *she tell her parents? What would they do to her?* to him? *He remembered one*

night when he'd been late getting Betty home—she was just fifteen, after all, just a sophomore—and she'd told him not to worry about it. She'd said her mother had just been elected president of the PTA, and that she was so busy now she never noticed what time her daughter got home. And her father, an accountant, was too tired when he got home from work to care about anything except watching TV and sleeping. And if they did get mad at her, she'd just cry and sulk a little and they'd get over it. Or else they'd end up fighting each other, instead of her. They did that a lot lately. But Betty couldn't cry and sulk her way out of this, could she?

And what about his parents? His mother? She still treated him like a kid in some ways—hugging and kissing him, catering to him, picking up his clothes. But in other ways, she acted like he was old enough to be a man. Like when he told her he and Betty were going steady; she just looked at him kind of funny, and said it was up to him. And his father. He liked *his father; he worked hard and was a success in his profession; but he was never really* there. *When Don had been suspended from school for smoking, his father had been too busy to come to school and talk to the vice principal about it, so his mother had had to handle it. And when he won an award in school, his father had been too busy to come then, too. Would he be too busy* now?

Somebody had to help. He couldn't handle this by himself. Somebody had to help.

He walked home slowly. It was late. He must have been walking for two or three hours. And he'd promised to call Betty back. But what could he say? He didn't know what to tell her. He knew a boy who'd taken a girl to Tijuana for an abortion, but he couldn't see himself and Betty doing that. He couldn't see any solution at all.

The lights were still on downstairs when he reached home. That wasn't unusual. His mother often stayed up late waiting for him to come home. She never waited up for his father, though, when he was out late. When he opened the front door, he saw both his parents in the living room, waiting for him. He couldn't remember that ever having happened in his life before—both his parents waiting for him, together. They must know. Betty must have panicked when he didn't call her, and told her parents, and they must have called his. He felt weak at the sight of both his parents confronting him, but also a sense of relief. They'd have to go somewhere from here. It wasn't just up to him or up to Betty now. Maybe their parents wouldn't know what to do either. But at least they'd have to talk about it. And somebody would have to do something.

Yet if he had expected them to be unified in their condemnation or support of him, he was disappointed. His mother was angry and overwrought about the things Betty's parents had said—that they might even bring rape charges against Don. She alternately castigated Betty for being no good, berated Don for having had anything to do with her, and virtually begged him to tell her that he wasn't, couldn't be the father. His father was less hysterical, but he was angry with Don for having been so stupid. His chief reaction, too, though, was condemnation of Betty. "No nice girl would have gone that far," he said. "We'll get you out of it somehow."

His parents' reactions closed off any avenue of approach for him to discuss his feelings, his sense of guilt, of loss, of ignorance, of fear, of frustration, or his desire to help Betty.

Who could he talk to? Who in the world would understand, would listen?

Betty wasn't at school the next day. He was relieved—he couldn't picture himself going up to her, talking to her, touching her. And that was stupid. He didn't like himself for feeling that way. Only a little while ago, they'd spent every spare moment together—they couldn't not *touch each other.*

And now—he didn't know what was happening to him. Everything inside himself seemed to be at war. Call her. Don't call her. You love her. You don't ever want to see her again. You want to help her. You want your father to handle things so you don't have to worry or think about what has happened.

At lunch time, in desperation, he finally asked Marilyn, Betty's best friend, to call her, telling Marilyn he and Betty had had a quarrel. Once he knew Betty was on the phone, he literally grabbed the phone from Marilyn and elbowed her out of the phone booth, then stood huddled miserably holding the receiver, not knowing what to say, feeling completely alone. Finally he said, "Betty, it's Don."

"Oh." The girl's voice was cold and remote.

"Listen," he said. "I'm—I'm sorry I didn't call back last night. I just didn't know what to say."

"I see," she said.

"Look," he implored, "I want to help, Bets. I really do. I just don't know what to do—or how—." He stopped and took a deep breath. "How did your parents take it?"

"Awful," she said. "And at first, they didn't even seem to care about me. *They were afraid of what everybody might think—our relatives, friends, the neighbors. They said I'd just have stay in the house so nobody would find out. Then they started in on each other. Dad said it was Mom's fault and Mom said it was his fault. They went back and forth for a while, and then they both turned on me and asked how I could do this to them. You know, like I'd purposely gotten pregnant just so I could make them both miserable."*

"Oh, Bets," he said miserably, "I should have been with you when you told them."

"No," she said, "I don't think so. Oh, maybe they'd have turned on you, instead of me or each other, but that wouldn't have helped. Anyhow, after they wore themselves out, they started thinking about me a little—and about the baby—how they might have to support it, how I'll probably have to leave school, whether—whether anybody *would ever want to marry me."*

"Listen, Bets. Do you—do you want *to get married? I've got my delivery job, you know. It wouldn't be enough, but maybe we could work it out some way."*

"I don't know, Don. I just don't know. I'm really just so mixed up I don't know what I—we—should do."

"Yeah," he agreed. "I know, I feel the same way." He paused, then said, "Look, do you remember Johnny and Marnie? He took her to Tijuana, and she—"

"No," she said, cutting him off sharply. "I don't want to do that. Besides, I'm almost positive it's too late."

"Okay," he said. "Sure. It was just one thing I thought of." There was a long, awkward silence, and finally he said, "Bets, what can *I do?"*

"I don't know," she said. "My mother's going to talk to someone today—some kind of agency. I hate the thought of going to strangers, but—well, I could see it was hard for her to call them, but she did it. So . . . we'll just wait and see. Okay?"

"Yeah, sure," he said. "Okay. I guess—I guess I'll be seeing you then, huh?"

"Yes," she said softly. "I'll be seeing you."

After he had hung up, he didn't know whether he felt better or worse. Certainly he didn't feel good. He didn't think he'd ever *feel good again. He had thought that if he could bring himself to ask her to marry him, that would settle it. He didn't want to get married, either, but it was supposed to be the thing to do, wasn't it?*

Nobody really seemed to know what to do.

Don's feelings of guilt and frustration were hardening into anger, and that night he fought with his parents. Why had they left him alone so much, he demanded. Why had they let him have the car? If he hadn't had the car it wouldnt' have happened. Why hadn't they forbidden him to go steady with Betty? Why didn't they even care what time he got home? Why didn't they get along better with each oher? Why couldn't he talk to them now?

He sensed that he was behaving childishly, that he was seeking to escape his own guilt by placing the blame on them, but he couldn't seem to help it. He finally ran to his room, slammed the door, and refused to talk to them at all.

Betty called him the next day, and told him that she and her mother had been to the agency, and that a social worker at the agency would like to see Don. She told him that her parents didn't particularly want Don involved any further; that they would rather she never have any occasion to see or talk to him again; but that the social worker had pointed out that, after all, Don was already so vitally involved that he should share the responsibility with her, both for his sake and hers.

Don agreed to go to the agency, but with a sense of futility and reluctance. He shared Betty's initial antipathy about discussing the problem with strangers and, beyond that, he virtually despaired of achieving understanding from anyone. But it appeared to be the only remaining course of action open to him.

1 Illegitimacy as a Social Problem

Illegitimacy has been a social problem for centuries. The number of illegitimate births increases steadily, the "pill" notwithstanding. In 1969, the number of unwed mothers nationally was estimated at 310,000. Approximately 135,000 were under 20 years of age.[1] Obviously, for each unwed mother, there is an unwed father, thus adding another 135,000 persons to those caught up in this complex drama. In addition, 175,000 women beyond the teen years gave birth to out-of-wedlock children, again, of course, with the involvement of a corresponding number of fathers. Thus, including the offspring, in a mere 12 months a minimum of some 930,000 human beings in the United States entered directly into the "unmarried parenthood" relationship.

These massive figures pertain only to illegitimate births. When we consider that many pregnant mothers—the total number is unknown—were aborted, or eluded official recognition of their dilemma, the staggering immensity of the problem becomes clear.

One basis for this rise in the number of illegitimate births is simply our continued population growth and the corresponding increase in the number of women of childbearing age. Beyond this, other factors are at work. Sexual relations between unmarried persons appear to be gaining greater acceptance. Such acceptance ends problematically, however, when the union leads to out-of-wedlock pregnancy. In present social practice, the attention is focused on the most tangible consequence—the child.

Although American sexual mores are undergoing broad changes, yielding greater freedom in sexual behavior outside marriage, the persons involved in out-of-wedlock births are still castigated. Punitive measures may be taken against the mother; often the child's rights under the law are beclouded; and the unmarried father may be pursued legally for financial support and possible criminal prosecution. About one in five children born out of wedlock are welfare recipients[2] and, when this is the case, the established community's concern is accentuated. Public assistance may be denied to the mother if a second illegitimate pregnancy occurs, and a jail sentence may even be imposed if the mother refuses to undergo sterilization. In 1967, a young New Jersey woman was prosecuted for fornication when it was discovered that she was pregnant with a child conceived out of wedlock.

Forbidding welfare support to a mother who has a second illegitimate child stems from the philosophy that the child's birth was the result of a deliberate, planned action. That mothers not on welfare rolls also have illegitimate children is ignored by those seeking to punish public welfare recipients. Further, as we shall see later in this chapter, it may be seriously doubted whether premeditation and purposeful action are, indeed, at the root of illegitimacy, and whether the present widely held view that this is so is realistic.

Preoccupation with Unmarried Motherhood and Widening Implications

Succeeding and overlapping problems that are not transitory but which have consequences that deeply affect many lives for years to come stem from the illicit sexual relationship, just as the circles from a pebble dropped in water succeed and overlap each other. The popular simplification that illegitimacy is an accident that can be prevented if there is easy access to contraceptives, though superficially comforting, is of doubtful validity.

While the acceptance of an open, frank approach to sex education has as one of its goals the reduction of undesired consequences of illicit sexual behavior—specifically, illegitimate births and venereal disease—the assumption that sex education will, per se, reduce these consequences has not yet been proven. To be successful, sex education must relate to the values of interpersonal relationships and concern for others.

Unfortunately, whenever illegitimacy is discussed the focus is, by and large, on the unmarried mother. It is she who is ostracized by her family and community, and on whom activity of all kinds is centered. Social agencies that serve unmarried mothers have seldom dealt with anyone other than the mother, her parents, and the out-of-wedlock child. In the typical "scenario," replayed endlessly over the years, unmarried mothers have retreated to maternity homes, have had their babies, and have eventually returned to society "as if nothing had happened." In a sense, the experience was treated as an isolated incident to be forgotten as quickly as possible following the birth of the baby —providing the child was placed for adoption. Isolating the unmarried mother from the day-by-day setting in which she lives, and helping her, after the baby is born, to forget the illegitimate pregnancy, fails to recognize her as a person and ignores the genuine complexity of the event.

Ruth Chaskel, former Director of the National Council on Illegitimacy in the United States, says: "The concept of the unmarried *family,* rather than professional preoccupation with the unmarried mother alone or the out-of-wedlock child in a vacuum, is steadily gaining ground."[3]

The need to push beyond the traditional services (that is, working exclusively with the unmarried mother and her problems) is currently being reviewed by many social agencies. One example of this widening concern is the family/community oriented position that is beginning to gain favor with such agencies. Beyond the unmarried father—the key concern in this book—we need to focus more attention upon providing services for the unmarried mother who keeps her child; not only material assistance, but help in meeting the social and emotional problems in her life. We need to know more about the development of the child reared in a fatherless family and about the special problems of the unmarried mother who takes on the dual role of mother *and* father.

We need to deepen our understanding of how the unmarried mother who gives her child for adoption integrates this experience into her later life adjustment. Although adoption provides a logical and hopeful solution for many children born out of wedlock, it is not an uncomplicated solution. Adoptive agencies throughout the country are beginning to see the need for providing more help to couples adopting children. In this connection, we recognize that one of the major problems facing many adoptive couples is how to handle their feelings about the child's natural parents. One way we can provide better service to such couples is to give them a greater understanding of the child's natural parents, *including the father.*

We can also provide better services for adoptive children by giving them meaningful background information concerning their natural father as well as their natural mother. Elizabeth Anglim, an authority on the adoption process, speaks forcefully on this point:

If we really believe that a child has a right to information about his natural parents and that a positive image offers him the best hope of security, we must begin to offer this image to the adoptive parents. For this, there are two basic requirements—first, a conviction about, and acceptance of, the principles involved and, second, the time required to put these into effect. If the first becomes part of our professional thinking, we will somehow, in spite of the growing pressures from all areas, find the time necessary to add another client to each case and, therefore, to furnish to many more adoptive children a realistic and more complete picture of their biological heritage and the reason their natural parents chose adoption for them. We have long counseled adoptive parents that they must be ready for the child's inevitable question: "Why did my mother give me up?" Now I hope we can help them to be free to hear and to be able to answer the inevitable next question: "But what about my father?"[4]

The Unmarried Father as a Participant

And what do we know, or *think* we know, about the unmarried father?

When the father is thought of at all, he is often imagined to be an older sophisticate who has lured a young innocent girl into a compromising situation. Thus the mother is viewed as a victim of circumstances and is to be pitied. This lets everyone "off the hook" very neatly. No one except the amorphous father, unseen, unheard, is to blame.

Or, perhaps the father is viewed as a sower of wild oats, and as such is surreptitiously regarded has having behaved in a manner that is to be expected of red-blooded youth. The woman who succumbs to his advances and becomes pregnant is then seen as one without morals who is reaping the "just deserts" of her dalliance. Fathers of unwed fathers frequently express this viewpoint, and add that paternity, therefore, cannot easily be established—"My son is just one of many." The implications in such attitudes is that relationships from which out-of-wedlock children are born are casual in nature and that no one attaches much meaning to them.

Consequently, unmarried fathers are expected to remove themselves from the scene—to conveniently fade away, if you will—when they are presumed to have caused a woman in an out-of-wedlock status to become pregnant. All eyes turn toward the mother. Concern for her feelings is paramount. She is the one who receives attention, medical and otherwise. She is the one who incurs bills for herself, for her parents, for the community. It is she with whom plans for the future are discussed. Any hostility she may harbor for the child's father is usually reinforced by her parents. Mention of him is skirted. It is as if he exists only in fantasy and is not a real person with needs, fears, doubts, and perhaps guilt feelings.

This separation of the father from the problem results in a paradox. On one hand, he is the "forgotten man." On the other hand, he is castigated by society if he fails to provide for support of the child. Again, this issue arises more frequently when the unmarried mother is on the relief rolls. The unmarried father is ignored but, at the same time, he serves as a handy scapegoat upon whom society and parents of unmarried mothers can vent their wrath and frustration. Thus, it must be observed that, in many instances, the unmarried father is overlooked as an integral participant in the drama of unmarried parenthood.

On the other hand, national organizations that concern themselves with the problem of illegitimacy have recently begun to recognize the need to provide services for unmarried fathers. The Child Welfare League of America, for example, in its *Standards for Services to Unmarried Parents*, states:

> The unmarried father, especially the adolescent, should have an opportunity for casework help. Social agencies offering counseling services, family welfare services, as well as specialized services for unmarried parents should *reach out* to the father more than they have in the past. They should specify services for unmarried fathers among those they offer. At the present time, little professional knowledge is available in the literature or from research about the unmarried father. Special efforts should be made to work with him and to develop studies regarding him.[5]

Demonstration Project—Reaching Unmarried Fathers

Recognition of the need to explore systematically the particular impact of illegitimate pregnancy on the unmarried father was based partly on the authors' social agency experience and partly on the factors and reflections recounted in the foregoing paragraphs. This recognition led to a proposal to conduct a three-year demonstration study. The proposal was approved, and partially financed, by the Children's Bureau of the United States Department of Health, Education, and Welfare. Vista Del Mar Child-Care Service, Los Angeles, and the Jewish Federation—Council of Greater Los Angeles were joint recipients of the grant. The former assumed responsibility for providing social work services and thus the needed contact with the unmarried parents; the latter assumed responsibility for the research aspects of the study.

The study undertook to: 1) develop a plan to "reach out" to unmarried fathers and to engage them in a relationship with the social workers; 2) ascertain the characteristics of unmarried fathers as a group—what they are like, what kinds of problems they have, etc.; 3) ascertain the effects of involving unmarried fathers in a casework relationship; and 4) develop methods for obtaining data in a systematic manner. The results of this study form the basis for the material presented in this book.

Although our emphasis in the study was on the unmarried father, we gathered information about unmarried mothers simultaneously. This made it possible to present a more meaningful picture of the unmarried father, particularly with reference to relationships between unmarried parents.

This study, like many that are done on any population served by a particular agency, was focused on a client group with its own characteristics, varying in some measure from client populations served elsewhere. The underlying forces operating here, however, were such that the conclusions may be generalized, with caution, to apply to populations of unmarried parents served by social agencies with a similar practice orientation. Other agencies are beginning to employ approaches comparable to those used at Vista Del Mar. For example, conclusions not unlike those stated here are being reached by the Natural Father Project of the West Covina District Office of the Los Angeles County Department of Adoptions; in the study, "The Juvenile Unwed Father," by the Youth Center of Philadelphia[6]; and in some of the findings of a New York study entitled, "Experiences of the Unwed Mother as a Parent."[7]

In the following pages, the unmarried father and his

problems will be highlighted, but the unmarried mother will not be ignored. Indeed, her characteristics and problems will often be considered in a manner parallel to that in which those of the father are considered. Unmarried parenthood is a partnership of sorts and it is within this context that this study of unmarried fathers was conducted.

Notes and References

1. Unpublished paper by Dr. Charles Gershenson, Director, Division of Research, Children's Bureau, Washington, D.C. Conference on Schoolage Pregnant Girls, Los Angeles, Calif., May 26, 1969. *Vital Statistics Report,* Vol. 15, No. 3, June 14, 1966, Washington, D.C., U. S. Department of Health, Education and Welfare, reports 275,700 illegitimate live births for 1964.
2. About one in five children born out of wedlock are recipients of public assistance (AFDC) as reported in "Illegitimacy and Dependency." *Health, Education and Welfare Indicators,* Washington, D.C.: U. S. Department of Health, Education and Welfare, 1963.
3. Ruth Chaskel. "Changing Patterns of Services for Unmarried Parents." *Social Casework,* January, 1968.
4. Elizabeth Anglim. "The Adopted Child's Heritage—Two Natural Parents." *Child Welfare, XLIV,* June, 1965.
5. *Child Welfare League of America Standards for Services to Unmarried Parents.* New York: Child Welfare League of America, Inc., 1960, p. 26.
6. Mignon Sauber and Elaine Rubinstein. "Experiences of the Unwed Mother as a Parent: A Longitudinal Study of Unmarried Mothers Who Keep Their First Born." New York: Research Department, Community Council of Greater New York, 1965.

7. Robert F. Perkins and Ellis S. Grayson. "The Juvenile Unwed Father." In *Effective Services for Unmarried Parents and Their Children: Innovative Community Approaches,* New York: National Council on Illegitimacy, 1968.

II The Study Plan

The objectives of the study* that is the basis of this book determined the final research design. Two objectives which sought to determine the effect of involving the unmarried father in a casework relationship influenced the decision to adopt an experimental method. These objectives were:

1. To determine what effect involving the unmarried father in a casework relationship has upon the decision made regarding the future of the child.
2. To determine what effect involvement of the unmarried father in a casework relationship has upon the unmarried mother and himself.

To study effect, it is necessary to provide services to one group of clients and to withhold the same services from another group of clients. This method may enable the researcher to relate the outcomes to the kinds of services being provided.

It was estimated that somewhat more than 100 unmarried mothers would come to Vista Del Mar for help in *each* of the three years projected for the data-gathering phase of the study. It was assumed that these cases would be numbered consecutively in order of date and time of intake [1 . . . (N), when N is approximately 100].

*This chapter answers questions of a technical nature for those readers who are interested in this aspect of the study.

For cases 1 and 2, 4 and 5, 7 and 8, etc., it was determined that every effort *would* be made to reach the father and to involve him in casework. These "experimental" cases were designated as Group I, determination: father to be reached.

For case 3, 6, 9, etc., the initial determination was made that the father would *not* be reached. These control cases were designated as Group II, determination: father *not* to be reached.

Group I was subdivided into *two* principal subgroups:

a. The cases in which, in accordance with initial determination, the father *was* reached and substantially participated in casework: Subgroup 1a, father was actually reached as per initial determination.
b. The cases in which efforts to reach the father failed: Subgroup 1b, father not reached in spite of initial determination.

Some modification of this design was required for the selection of the control groups. Caseworkers pointed out that occasionally a case labeled "control" was sufficiently idiosyncratic to require its designation as "experimental." For example, in those instances where the couple married prior to the birth of the child, and the mother continued her relationship with the agency, it was important that both parents be seen.* A procedure was established whereby exceptions could be made. This procedure was highly formal-

*An unmarried mother was defined as a woman who conceived a child out of wedlock, whether or not she subsequently married the unmarried father or someone else. If she was already married to someone else and was impregnated by someone other than her husband, she was still considered an unmarried mother. Essentially, the same criteria were applied to males who fathered out-of-wedlock children.

ized and required approval of the social work administrator and both members of the research team.

This flexibility in research procedures points up the understanding reached between caseworkers and researchers. It was understood from the beginning that agency objectives and practices would not become secondary to the research method. The agency, Vista Del Mar Child-Care Service, had a commitment to clientele that could not be interrupted or interfered with if the agency was to continue service as provided for in its bylaws. A corollary to this principle was necessary, however, to permit the research to proceed. Caseworkers had to modify certain procedures in order to permit data to be gathered as required by the research design.

Reaching points of agreement between the social workers and the researchers in regard to method was sometimes a lengthy process. As Wolins points out,[1] withholding services from clients is frequently unacceptable to social workers, particularly when they are already convinced that they are providing services that are essential to the well-being of their clients. The social workers, generally, were nonaccepting in regard to the establishment of control groups. For approximately six years prior to the study, the agency had been actively reaching out to unmarried fathers. Although reaching out methods became more formalized during the study, the social workers entered into the study phase of the project with a high degree of sophistication in working with unmarried fathers. Experience gained over this six-year period had generally convinced the social workers that unmarried fathers and unmarried mothers both benefitted when the unmarried father was engaged in a social work relationship. Hence, as a group, they had difficulty in accepting the notion that some unmarried fathers would not be seen. Many joint sessions of social workers and researchers were held to explore this point and, even though eventual resolution of the problem occurred, some misgivings lingered on for some of the social workers. In spite of this, fewer exceptions were made for seeing "control" cases than was projected (as shown in Table 1), suggesting that the social workers exerted professional, disciplined control in selecting cases for exception.

Another objective of the study was to identify attributes of the unmarried father, particularly his psychosocial attributes. We wanted to know what kind of a person he was and what kinds of problems he faced.

Although the study focus was on the unmarried father, the decision was made to obtain comparable information on unmarried mothers. The study team was in a unique position: unmarried fathers studied were partners of unmarried mothers receiving social work counseling service simultaneously by the same agency. We reasoned that profiles of unmarried fathers would have more meaning if

TABLE 1. *Projection of Success in Reaching Unmarried Fathers and Actual Experience in Reaching Them*

	Fathers to Be Seen		*Fathers Not to Be Seen*	
	Projected %	*Actual* %	*Projected* %	*Actual* %
Seen	67	50	30	26
Not seen	33	50	70	74
Total	100	100	100	100
(No. of cases)	(134)	(153)	(66)	(73)
	(X^2 4.65, df=1; $p<.05$; significant)		(X^2 0.56, df=1; $p<.90$; not significant)	

compared with profiles of unmarried mothers. The research finding that an unmarried mother/unmarried father constellation exists supports this initial hypothesis.

Data from which descriptions of unmarried parents were derived came from three sources: 1) a member of the research staff met with the unmarried mothers and fathers to administer a battery of psychological and sociological tests; 2) unmarried mothers and fathers provided background data about themselves by completing an Information Form; and 3) social workers supplied considerable information through completion of the Standardized Case Recording Form (see Appendix). During the early phase of the study, social workers expressed concern that client-worker relationships would be jeopardized by the introduction of an "outsider," i.e., the researcher. In addition, some concern was expressed that the process of obtaining psychological data would "scare off" the unmarried father and thereby result in inconclusive interviews. Again, through meetings of the project staff, these issues were resolved, and the study proceeded according to plan.

Data were gathered on 222 unmarried mothers and 96 unmarried fathers. In some tables, the number of unmarried mothers appears as 226. This is due to the fact that in three cases we had multiple fathers involved with the same mother (three fathers with one unmarried mother and two fathers in two separate cases with one unmarried mother), thus increasing our unmarried mother/unmarried combinations by four. Variations in the numbers of cases are also due to the fact that information on all variables was not available for all subjects.

Erik Erikson's concept of identity diffusion was selected as the theoretical base for studying unmarried parents.[2] Clark Vincent's references to the applicability of Erikson's theory tended to reinforce our decision.[3] Dr. Deschin, in her study, *Teenagers and Venereal Disease,* also referred to this concept:

> Some of the diffuseness in . . . responses is a characteristic of adolescence inasmuch as, during this period, young people are struggling between achieving their own identity and relating it to the meaningful adults in their social situation. Nevertheless, it is confirmation of the impression gained from the interviewing; namely, that the teenagers are more troubled than many of the clinic personnel seemed to realize. For example, it is striking that almost a third should not be able to identify with anyone and that twenty-three percent had not found anyone in their environment with whom they can identify.[4]

Through experience at Vista Del Mar, we were acutely aware that a disproportionate number of our couples were interfaith units. Many were either young adults or pre-adults and were, therefore, still in the formative stages of development. We also noted that many unmarried parents favored placing their children for adoption and were not interested in solidifying relationships through marriage. These observations suggested that our subjects were searching for something—an identity, perhaps—and, from this suggestion, the relevance of Erik Erikson's concept of "identity versus identity diffusion" emerged as a theoretical base. Indicators of identity diffusion, as extrapolated from Erikson's work[5] are:

1. Inability to function in a controlled society.
2. Inability to engage in a mature relationship with others.

3. Inner despair—a lack of sense of knowing where one is going.
4. Inclination not to want recognition or approval from others.
5. Repudiation of societal norms.
6. Excessive self-love.

Some of the instruments chosen to gather information concerning these indicators were: 1) the California Psychological Inventory, which focuses on skills and attitudes necessary for social functioning; 2) attitudinal scales developed by Jessor, designed to measure personal disjunctions and the degree to which individuals regard a typical behavior as deviant; and 3) reports of behavior and attitude as supplied by caseworkers. In addition, we also reasoned that we would find problems pertaining to the interpersonal relationships between the unmarried fathers and unmarried mothers, and we gathered this information from a Standardized Case Recording Form to be described later.

In addition to the above theoretical formulations, some assumptions that helped guide our selection of data to be gathered were based upon experience. These assumptions included:

1. In a sense, the out-of-wedlock child is conceived in fantasy. Therefore, the development of a reality orientation for the unmarried father as well as the unmarried mother is a significant aspect of casework.
2. Particularly in teen-age illegitimacy, the roles of the parents (or other authority figures) of the unmarried couple are important. Therefore, the unmarried parents' relationships to their parents are appropriate focal points for practice and study.

3. Making decisions about the future of the child constitutes a specific key problem for all concerned. Therefore, the decision-making process is a suitable focus for casework and evaluation.
4. The reaction of the unmarried parents to the pregnancy and the infant is symptomatic of their basic life problems and modes of adjustment. Therefore, casework should be specifically concerned with these deeper, long-range dynamics as well as with necessary immediate solutions.
5. Although initially assertive procedures may be required to reach the unmarried father, a mutually positive relationship eventually develops between him and the male caseworker.
6. The involvement of the unmarried father in casework will serve both him and the unmarried mother in the movement from fantasy to reality, in the improved handling of parental and authority relationships, in more effective decision-making concerning the child, and in the development of a more mature approach to the general problems of living.

To study effectiveness of casework intervention, we were faced with the necessity of evaluating what happens during the casework process. Because of the dearth of standardized instruments for measurement of the effectiveness of casework, we devised our own instrument. This was termed a Standardized Case Recording Form, which the caseworker filled out at two points in time—at an early point in the casework process and at termination of the casework process. This instrument, primarily closed-end in nature, was developed during the tooling-up phase of the study, and followed a series of interviews between the caseworker and a member of the resarch staff. The closed-end questions were based on the kinds of responses usually given to open-end questions. To provide an opportunity for caseworkers to supplement information from responses to closed-end items, sections for comments were provided in various places on the forms.

In order to identify the population under study, it was deemed important to obtain demographic data. To meet the replication requirements of the design, Clark Vincent's Information Form, which explores patterns of family relationships, was employed. Some unmarried parents answered all questions, some answered only some of the questions, and some did not participate in filling out the Information Form. Psychological and sociological tests were administered only if the unmarried parents agreed to participate. Some refused, and others were unable to do so, generally because of short-term contact with the agency. Hence, the number of cases in the tables varies.

Another difficulty that arose in connection with implementing the design was that of obtaining information, particularly from unmarried fathers whose relationship with the agency was short-lived. We found, for example, that once the subject severed his relationship with the caseworker, it was practically impossible to bring about his return to the agency to fill in required forms or to take the various psychological tests. As the project progressed, we found some success in beginning the data gathering at the first or second interview. Contrary to worker expectations, this change in sequence did not seem to affect establishment of a casework relationship. In fact, in some instances, the involvement of the subject in providing such information seemed to strengthen the relationship and, in a sense, brought about a personal commitment on the part of the subject, which continued throughout the project. In some instances, we were able to gather pieces of information but frequently were unable to gather all the data required.

Attempts to contact unmarried fathers who did not live in the community did not prove fruitful. Some of our unmarried mothers had come from other communities (these we termed non-local) to have their babies, and planned to return to their home community once the baby was delivered and placed for adoption. Although we attempted to reach some of the fathers through letters and telephone calls, this did not prove to be satisfactory. We considered asking agencies in other communities to assist by interviewing these unmarried fathers and obtaining the information needed. This method was discarded because of the administrative and technical problems involved.

The six full-time caseworkers (three male workers who saw unmarried fathers and three female workers who worked with unmarried mothers) continued with the project from its inception until all data gathering was complete. Through frequent meetings with the research staff, caseworkers carrying direct responsibility for providing services to clients were involved in all phases of the research project.

Notes and References

1. Martin Wolins. "Measuring the Effect of Social Work Intervention." In *Social Work Research,* ed. by Norman A. Polansky, Chicago: University of Chicago Press, 1960.
2. Erik H. Erikson. "The Problem of Ego Identity." *Journal of the American Psychological Association, IV*, 1956, pp. 56-121.
3. Clark Vincent. *Unmarried Mothers.* New York: The Free Press, 1961, p. 254.

4. Cecia S. Deschin. *Teenagers and Venereal Disease: A Sociological Study, Atlanta.* Washington, D.C.: U. S. Department of Health, Education and Welfare, 1961.
5. Erik H. Erikson. *Psychological Issues,* Vol. I, No. 1. New York: International Universities Press, Inc., 1959.

III Some Basic Facts

The incidence of unmarried parenthood by age group of unmarried mothers seen by the study agency, Vista Del Mar,* was compared with unmarried mothers nationally (Table 2).**

TABLE 2. *Ages of Unmarried Mothers in the Study and in the United States*

Age	*Study* %		*United States** %	
Under 15	.8	57.2	2.1	41.3
15-19	56.4		39.2	
20-24	28.9		31.8	
25-29	10.1		13.7	
30-34	2.2		4.2	
35-39	1.6		1.3	
40 and over	0.0		7.6	
Total	100.0		100.0**	
(No. of cases)***	(222)		(259,400)	

*Bureau of Census, *Illegitimate Live Births, 1963.*
**Rounded to 100.0%.
***Refer to Chapter II for further details regarding the study design.

*The terms "study agency," "agency," "Vista Del Mar Child-Care Service" or "Vista Del Mar" are used interchangeably.
**When not otherwise noted, figures and tables refer to present study.

The age comparisons are gross but, in spite of differences, show substantially similar trends. In the study more than half, and in the United States somewhat less than half, of the unmarried mothers were under twenty, but a considerable group, some 14 percent in the study and nearly double this proportion in the most recent available U. S. total, were twenty-five years old or over. This contradicts the common view that practically all illegitimacy is confined to teen-agers.

The national data given in Table 2 and the state figures presented in Table 3 include all unmarried mothers regardless of whether or not they had contact with a social agency. But there are differences in the data from the two sources. The state figures, for example, report the ages of unmarried parents who place the child for adoption. Na-

TABLE 3. *Ages of Unmarried Mothers and Unmarried Fathers in the Study and in the State of California*

Age	*Unmarried Fathers*		*Unmarried Mothers*	
	Vista Del Mar %	*Calif.* %	*Vista Del Mar* %	*Calif.* %
19 and under	28.3	10.2	57.2	29.7
20-24	44.1	28.5	28.9	34.2
25-29	17.2	24.6	10.1	19.2
30-34	6.2	13.6	2.2	8.8
35-39	2.6	8.7	1.6	4.6
40 and over	1.5	6.0	0.0	2.1
Unknown	0.0	8.4	0.0	1.3
Total	100.0*	100.0	100.0	100.0
(No. of cases)	(96)	(4176)	(222)	(4176)

*Rounded to 100.0%.

tional figures report ages of unmarried mothers as a group, whether or not adoption services are used. Still, the comparative patterns are worth our attention, as a general guide to placing the study findings in a more general context.

California statistics on age include that of unmarried fathers as well as unmarried mothers, a statistic not presently collected nationally. Table 3 compares ages of unmarried study parents with ages of unmarried parents for California, adapted from statistics compiled by the Department of Social Welfare of the State of California.[1]

In California, the greatest percentage of unmarried fathers is in the age group 20 to 24. Next are those in the age group 25 to 29, then 30 to 34, and fourth, teen-agers. At Vista Del Mar Child-Care Service, the greatest percentage of unmarried fathers was in the age group 20 to 24. Next were the teen-agers, followed by the age groups 25 to 29 and 30 to 34.

It would appear that teen-agers accounted for a greater percentage of unmarried fathers in this study than they do in the state of California as a whole. This may have been due to heightened family concern for the young unmarried father, which generated additional pressures to respond to services, including child placement, offered by an agency.

In California, the greatest percentage of unmarried mothers is in the age group 20 to 24. Next are teen-agers, followed by those in the age group 25 to 29, and fourth, those in the age group 30 to 34. At Vista Del Mar Child-Care Service, the greatest percentage of unmarried mothers are in the teen-age group, followed consecutively by age categories 20 to 24, 25 to 29, and 30 to 34.

Unmarried teen-age mothers who are in need of help in dealing with parenthood are more apt than those in other age groups to seek the service of a social agency, often at the direction of their parents. Thus a greater number of teen-agers than others come to the attention of agencies throughout the country. This is reflected in the difference in age groupings for unwed parents in the study group and in the state of California. Still, unmarried parenthood is clearly much more than a teen-age phenomenon.

Facts and Fiction

A stereotype of the unmarried father described earlier —a considerably older male who seduces an innocent young girl—is shown by the findings (Table 4) to be fiction. Sixty-nine percent of the couples were within four years of each

TABLE 4. *Age Differentials of Unmarried "Couples" in the Study*

Differential	%	
UM* and UF** same age	3.2	
UM 2 years or less younger	36.3	61.1 (first three rows)
UM 3-4 years younger	21.6	
UM 5-6 years younger	15.8	
UM 7 or more years younger	11.5	
UM 2 years or less older	5.2	
UM 3-4 years older	3.2	
UM 5-6 years older	1.1	
UM 7 or more years older	2.1	
Total	100.0	
(No. of cases)	(190)***	

*UM = unmarried mother.
**UF = unmarried father.
***Excludes 36 cases where ages of fathers were unknown.

other in age. Furthermore, in 61 percent of the cases, the unmarried father was no more than four years older than the unmarried mother. Based on these figures, patterns of age differential closely approximate those for married couples!

There were no significant class differentials between the unmarried parents in the study (Table 5). That is, the unmarried father was not the "wealthy" man who seduced the "poor" girl who was presumably overwhelmed by the attentions of someone whose status was above her own.

Several procedures were used to determine the subjects' "social class." Social class of parents of unmarried parents was computed to identify unmarried parents' social class position when: 1) subjects were minors; and 2) subjects were no longer minors but were dependent on family, e.g., college students. Social class was computed for the unmarried parents themselves when they were living in an independent or marital status.[2]

Approximately 17 percent of the unmarried mothers and

TABLE 5. *Social Class of Unmarried Parents in the Study (Utilizing Hollingshead's Formula)*

Social Class	*Fathers* %	*Mothers* %
Upper-upper	0	2.8
Lower-upper	20.0	14.9
Upper-middle	28.3	34.0
Upper-lower	46.7	42.6
	5.0	5.7
Total	100.0	100.00
(No. of cases)	(60)	(141)

20 percent of the unmarried fathers came from the upper class, and 77 percent and 75 percent, respectively, from middle class. Very few unmarried parents (5 percent) were from the lower class, thus disputing the stereotype that illegimacy occurs almost exclusively in the low levels of society.*

By way of further note on this theme, the study findings suggest that illegitimacy is not to be equated with lack of education (see Table 6). Approximately 70 percent of the unmarried parents, both mothers and fathers, had completed four years of high school or more. This contrasts with a roughly comparable average of 49.3 percent for white males and 51.2 percent for white females among the total U. S. population. When one considers that 57.2 percent of

TABLE 6. *Education of Unmarried Parents in the Study Group*

Amount of Education	*Fathers* %	*Mothers* %
Less than 2 years high school	6.6	5.1
2-3 years high school	25.3	22.9
4 years high school	25.3	40.2
3 years college or less but some college	33.3	27.9
4 years college or more	9.3	3.9
Total	100.0*	100.0
(No. of cases)	(175)	(179)

*Rounded to 100.0%.

*Interpretation of these findings requires recognition of the fact that the study group came from a select population. Vista Del Mar is a sectarian agency whose clients are drawn from the Jewish population in the Los Angeles community, and which serves a predominantly middle-class clientele.

the unmarried mothers and 28.3 percent of the unmarried fathers were eighteen years old or younger, the number who had completed high school appears particularly high for the study group. The population of unmarried parents studied were scholastic achievers, at least as measured by ability to complete and continue schooling, and had attained educational levels above the national average.

Marital Status

Another stereotype is the notion that out-of-wedlock children are invariably born to mothers who have never been married. This is not borne out by statistics from the state of California (see Table 7) where approximately 54

Table 7. *Unmarried Mothers' Marital Status at Time Agency Was Contacted*

Marital Status of UM's	*Vista Del Mar* %	*California* %
Never married	80.2	45.8
Married	0.9	26.1
Widowed	-	1.4
Divorced	10.0	12.4
Interlocutory decree	-	3.4
Separated	0.9	7.8
Annulled	1.3	0.8
Illegal marriage*	2.2	0.0
Married after conception	4.4	0.0
Total	100.0**	100.0**
(No. of cases)	(222)	(4,176)

*Marriages obtained in Mexico by U.S. teen-agers. In most cases, these marriages are illegal in the U.S.

**Rounded to 100.0%.

percent of the children born out of wedlock are born to women who are either widowed, divorced, separated, or married to someone other than the father of the child. However, in view of the study group's youthfulness, the predominance of girls who had never been married is not surprising.

As to the marriage experiences of unmarried couples in the study, we found that, at the time of the illegitimate conception, neither partner had ever been married in 53 percent of the cases. (In 18 percent of the cases, information on the unmarried father's current or previous marital status was not available.) Of the remaining cases, both unwed parents had had some marital experience (see Table 8).

These statistics suggest that illegitimate births are by no means confined to the maritally innocent, though the unmarried are indeed most frequently encountered. The data suggest further that illegitimacy occurs among couples who, in many instances, are familiar with birth control methods.

For fathers seen at the agency and included in the *study* (N=96), marital status is shown in Table 9. (Similar data for other comparable groups are unavailable.)

The proportions of unmarried fathers in the various marital status categories were much the same as for unmarried mothers except for a high proportion of "now married" among the fathers (see Table 9-A).

Adoptive Status

It is evident from Table 10 that a very small proportion of unmarried parents, especially unmarried fathers, were themselves adopted. Thus, contrary to occasional folklore,

TABLE 8. *Marital Status of Unmarried Mother – Unmarried Father Partnerships, Vista Del Mar Study*

Marital Status of Couple	%
Both married (to someone else)	0.0
Both divorced	2.7
Both never married	53.1
Unmarried mother,* married; unmarried father, single**	0.4
Unmarried mother, single; unmarried father, married	8.4
Unmarried mother, divorced; unmarried father, single	3.5
Unmarried mother, single; unmarried father, divorced	7.1
Illegally married to each other***	2.2
Married to each other	4.4
No data on unmarried father	18.2
Total	100.0
(No. of cases)	(226)

*Mothers and fathers of out-of-wedlock children are designated "Unmarried Mothers" (UM) and "Unmarried Fathers" (UF) throughout this book, even though they may in reality be married, divorced, single or widowed.

**Single means "never married."

***Marriage considered illegal in California.

it is unlikely that being adopted oneself is a significant factor—unconscious or otherwise—predisposing to illegitimacy and thus to a repetition of the adoption cycle.

TABLE 9. *Unmarried Fathers' Marital Status at Time Agency Was First Contacted*

Marital Status of UF's	%
Never married	73.9
Married	5.2
Divorced	9.4
Illegal marriage to UM	5.2
Married to UM after conception	6.3
Total	100.0
(No. of cases)	(96)

TABLE 9-A. *Comparative Marital Status of Unmarried Mothers and Unmarried Fathers at Time Agency Was First Contacted*

Marital Status	*Unmarried Fathers* %	*Unmarried Mothers* %
Never married	73.9	80.2
Now married	5.2	0.9
Previous marriage or other marital status	20.9	18.9
Total	100.0	100.0
(No. of cases)	(96)	(222)

RECIDIVISM

A common stereotype is that once unmarried persons have had an out-of-wedlock child, they tend to repeat this experience.

Both partners in approximately 71 percent of the cou-

TABLE 10. *Percentages of Unmarried Parents Who Were Adopted Children*

Adopted	*Unmarried Fathers* %	*Unmarried Mothers* %
Yes	2.1	4.9
No	96.9	93.3
Don't know	1.0	1.8
Total	100.0	100.0
(No. of cases)	(96)	(222)

ples studied were experiencing parenthood for the first time. In 29 percent of the cases, one or both partners had had experience in the conception of an out-of-wedlock child. Of all the unmarried mother seen (222), 28 percent had conceived more than one out-of-wedlock child, the range being from two to four such pregnancies. Some 12 percent of the unmarried fathers had been involved in two or more pregnancies.

It is apparent from Table 11 that out-of-wedlock pregnancy within the study group was more often than not a one-time phenomenon, though some degree of recidivism was evident. At any rate, there was no evidence that in the majority of instances the predicament of the unmarried father and his partner reflected a steady pattern of promiscuous liaisons with indiscriminately selected partners. In fact, as will be pointed out in greater detail later, the majority of both the unmarried mothers and fathers tended to view their relationship as one of love or friendship. Less than 10 percent of the mothers and 17 percent of the fathers viewed the relationship as casual. Mostly, it was not a case of "love 'em and leave 'em" on the part of the fathers.

Table 11. *Incidence of Out-of-Wedlock Pregnancy for 79 Unmarried Couples*

Number of Pregnancies	%
1st pregnancy for each (UM & UF)	70.9
2nd pregnancy for UM, none previous for UF	10.1
2nd pregnancy for UF, none previous for UM	6.3
2nd pregnancy for each	6.3
Other combinations	6.3
Total	100.0*
(No. of cases)	(79)

*Rounded to 100.0%.

The relationship had some meaning and involved some commitment on their part as well as on the part of the mother.

Notes and References

1. J. M. Wedemeyer. *Independent Adoptions in California in 1962: Comparison of Adoptions by Relatives and by Non-Relatives. (Research Theories—Report No. 23)*, Sacramento: State of California Department of Social Welfare, April, 1965, pp. 9 and 10.
2. Social class was ascertained using Hollingshead's formula. August B. Hollingshead, *Two Factor Index of Social Class*, New Haven, 1957.

IV The Unmarried Father—Reachable

"They'll run when you try to catch them."
"They don't care about the mother. They won't bother talking to a social worker."
"She isn't going to tell you anything about him."
"She won't give his name."
"How can you find out who he is? Chances are that many could have been the father."

These are but a few of the remarks made to Vista Del Mar staff when the suggestion was made that we try to reach unmarried fathers and to learn more about them. Incredulity that an unmarried mother would consent to name the father of her child, or that he would admit to being the father, was expressed by lay and professional persons alike. They found it hard to believe that unmarried fathers would seek help from a social agency, or could even be induced to do so. Many were frankly skeptical that unmarried fathers had problems anyway; a typical observation was, "It's the mother who's left 'holding the bag'—she's the one who is having the baby."

The staff at Vista Del Mar, however, has ascertained that, in most cases, unmarried mothers *will* name the father, and that, if he lives in the area, the father *will* respond to a social agency's invitation to discuss the situation facing him and the others involved.

Naming the Unmarried Father

Before the social worker can expect the unmarried mother to name the child's father, the worker* must be comfortable in seeking such information. An attitude of reticence, or an indication that such information is unimportant, irrelevant, or embarrassing, is likely to be sensed by the mother. Thus, she may respond by professing ignorance or by avoiding the question in other ways.

In one instance, a worker from another agency made a telephone request that an unmarried mother be accepted by Vista Del Mar. In the course of the conversation, the Vista Del Mar social worker asked, "What is the name of the father?" There was an audible gasp at the other end of the line. After recovering her composure, the referring worker hesitatingly replied, "Just a moment." She could then be overheard saying to the mother, "You don't know the father's name, do you?" The mother's response was, "No." Subsequently, this unmarried mother readily and eagerly discussed the father with the Vista Del Mar caseworker.

The attitude shown by the worker from the referral agency in the case cited above suggests again that the unmarried father is often visualized as an untouchable. Further, he is frequently regarded merely as a symbol rather than as a real person with positive as well as negative qualities. Except for the few instances when the mother's sexual activity had been indiscriminate and promiscuous, our workers found that unmarried mothers usually had had quite a long acquaintance with the father. It was natural,

*The terms "social worker," "caseworker," and "worker" refer to the trained professional staff members of the agency (Vista Del Mar Child-Care Service). Both male and female social workers took part in the project, with male workers being assigned to the unmarried fathers.

therefore, for the caseworker (usually a woman) to review with the unmarried mother those attributes in the father that she may have admired or at least accepted. It then became quite easy to ask in a matter-of-fact manner, "And what is the name of the father?" This question was frequently raised during the initial interview.

Not all of the unmarried mothers in the study named the father on the first interview, and some never did. However, in 92 percent of the 226 cases of unmarried mothers, the unmarried mother named the unmarried father. It is evident that seeking the name of the father in a non-judgmental, non-anxiety-producing manner generally assures that it will be given.

Perhaps in the foregoing discussion the process of obtaining the name of the unmarried father has been oversimplified. In many instances, merely asking the question elicited the desired response, but some of the unmarried mothers refused to answer at first. Sometimes, particularly when the mother was a teen-ager, her parents objected to this question and were inclined to resist giving the name. Perhaps this was their attempt to deny the existence of the father, a denial that enabled them to treat the experience as fantasy-based and accidental. Or it may have expressed their feeling that the boy had "already done enough harm" to their daughter—why bring him in now and prolong their agony? In still other instances, the unmarried mother's parents were most anxious to name the father with the motive of heaping punishment upon him, either verbal or legal. In the few instances in which the unmarried mother had completely rejected the unmarried father, she generally refused to name him. Failure to name was not failure to know, as was shown in the case of Joan.

Joan, a young woman in her early twenties, came from the East Coast to Vista Del Mar to have her baby. She stated that she was on the threshold of a promising career and had arranged, under some pretext, to take an extended leave of absence. Her desire was to place the baby for adoption and then return to the East where she could continue with her career. She had not told the father about the baby and, furthermore, she had terminated the relationship with him by deliberately creating a scene. The unmarried father clearly did not fit into her plans; she had completely eliminated him from her life, and she was taking no chances that he would be brought back into the picture. We found that it was girls like Joan, who came long distances to have their babies, who were most unlikely to name the father.

Reaching the Unmarried Father

Once the name of the unmarried father was known, the next step was to reach him and encourage him to come to the agency for a conference with a social worker.

Based on the assumption that a more-or-less positive relationship exists between unmarried parents, project staff decided that the following conditions should prevail in reaching unmarried fathers:

1. Willingness of the unmarried mother to permit the agency to interview the unmarried father. This was paramount, and the decision was made to seek out the father only if the unmarried mother agreed.
2. The caseworker was to seek the unmarried mother's assistance in bringing the unmarried father to visit the agency.

To assure that social workers would be successful in reaching unmarried fathers, the following relevant principles were outlined:

1. The social worker should be aware of his own attitudes, beliefs, and prejudices regarding the possibilities and importance of involving the unmarried father.
2. The social worker should be concerned that constructive involvement of the unmarried father begins when the unmarried mother is encouraged to help establish a link between him and the agency.
3. The social worker should recognize that the ambivalent attitude of the unmarried father and mother toward each other enables him to utilize the positive aspects of the couple's relationship in initially involving them in ongoing casework.
4. The social worker must be prepared to introduce the concept that various benefits for all concerned, including personal growth and self-help, would come about by facing the situation rather than by running away from it.

Not only was it essential to work with the unmarried mothers to bring about the involvement of the fathers, but it was also frequently necessary to work with the mother's parents, some of whom resisted the idea that "the boy" should be seen. The following arguments are among those used to bring about acceptance of the idea (by the unmarried mother, her parents, or both) that the father should be involved:

1. The onus of total responsibility should be taken from the girl and shared by the father.

2. Assessing the relationship between the unmarried couple is better accomplished in the open, using the helping controls provided by the agency's professional staff.
3. A better and more wholesome opportunity for helping the girl resolve her feelings can be provided.
4. A better decision concerning the future of the baby is possible.
5. The girl's future plans can be more realistically discussed.

Agreement to the father's involvement carried with it knowledge on the part of the unmarried mother that some form of communication (direct or through caseworkers) with the father would occur during the pregnancy period.

Caseworkers at Vista Del Mar proceeded on the assumption that agreement by the unmarried mother to help get the father involved with the agency would generally be accompanied by success in reaching him. Furthermore, ready agreement on the part of the unmarried mother to do this would bring about greater participation by the father than when agreement was given reluctantly.

Seventy-three percent of the unmarried mothers in the study agreed to involve the fathers in an agency relationship. Of those agreeing, a considerable majority agreed readily and a minority agreed reluctantly (see Table 12).

As may be seen in Table 13, in the 106 cases in which the father was reached, 81 percent of the mothers agreed readily and 19 percent agreed reluctantly to involving the fathers. For the 120 unmarried fathers who were not reached, involvement was not sought for 43.3 percent, or 52 of the cases. Of the remainder, 21 percent of the mothers agreed readily, 12 percent agreed reluctantly, and 67 percent did not agree to involvement.

TABLE 12. *Percentages of Unmarried Mothers Who Agreed and Who Did Not Agree to Unmarried Father's Involvement with the Agency (Eliminating Control Where Involvement Was Not Sought*)*

Attitude	%	
Agreed to involvement	73.5	
Reluctantly		16.0
Readily		57.5
Did not agree to involvement	26.5	
Total	100.0	
(No. of cases)	(174)	

*By study design, involvement was not sought in 52 cases, or 15% of the total.

From Table 13 and Figure 1, it can be seen that success in reaching the unmarried father was directly associated with the mother's agreement that he be reached.

Once the mother agreed to the father's involvement with the agency, the next step was to enlist her active support in bringing this about. Taking an active part assumed many different forms. In some instances, the unmarried mother actually brought the unmarried father to the agency, although this was the exception rather than the rule. In other instances, she talked to the father and urged him to phone or write the agency for an appointment. In still other instances, she asked him to accept an appointment that had been made by the caseworker.

Sixty-six percent of the unmarried mothers actively aided in bringing the unmarried father to the agency. Those who did aid, however, were apt to be mothers who lived in the (local) Greater Los Angeles area. Those who were from

TABLE 13. *Relationship Between Unmarried Mother's Agreement to Father's Involvement and Success in Reaching Unmarried Fathers*

Success in Reaching Unmarried Father	Unmarried Mother's Attitude			
	Agreed		*Did Not*	*Involvement*
	Readily %	*Reluctantly* %	*Agree* %	*Not Sought* %
Reached	81.1	18.9	0.0	0.0
Not reached	11.7	6.6	38.3	43.3

Total % reached	*(No. of cases)*
100.0	(106)*
Total % not reached 100.0**	(120)
(Total no. of cases)	(226)

*Includes 10 unmarried fathers reached by letter or phone only.
**Rounded to 100.0%.

outside the area (non-local) were least likely to directly assist in involving the unmarried fathers. Seventy-seven percent of the local unmarried mothers actively aided in bringing the father to the agency, but only 35 percent of those from out of town did so (see Table 14 and Figure 2).

Two conclusions may be drawn from these findings:

1. The non-local unmarried mother, by her very action in leaving her home community, may have excluded (consciously or unconsciously) the unmarried father from sharing the knowledge of her predicament.
2. Because of logistic problems, the agency worker may have been less likely to expect involvement of the non-local unmarried father. Thus, the worker may

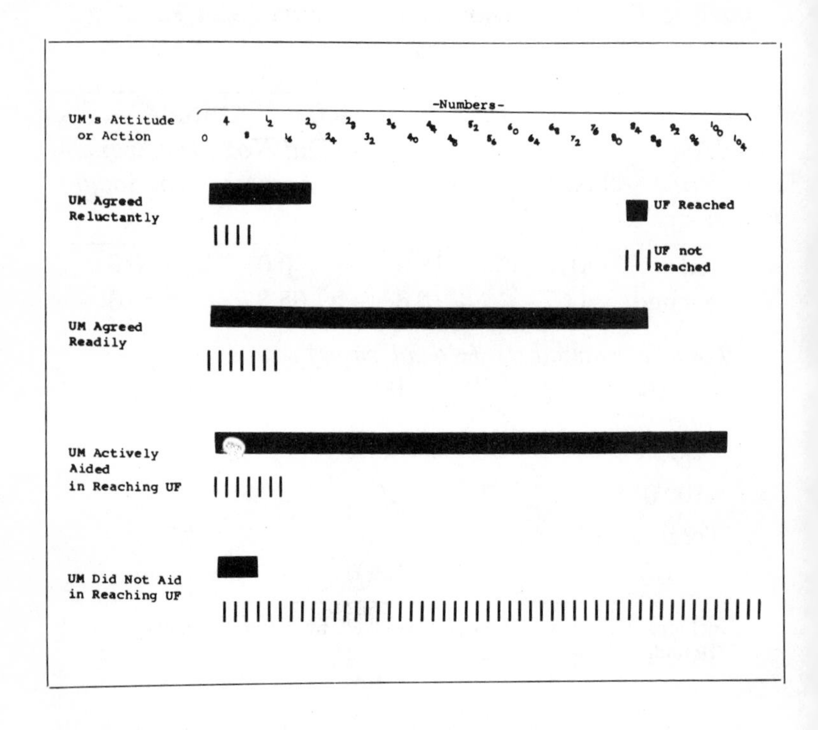

FIGURE 1. *Relationship of Numbers of Unmarried Fathers Reached to Agreement and Assistance of Unmarried Mothers*

have been less specific in identifying the potential benefits of the unmarried father's participation.

When the unmarried mother helped to reach the unmarried father, 94.3 percent of these were reached. When the unmarried mother did not aid, only 12.1 percent of the unmarried fathers were reached.

Table 14. *Extent to Which Local and Non-Local Unmarried Mothers Participated Actively in Involving the Unmarried Fathers with the Agency*

Mother's Residence	*Actively Aided* %	*Did not Actively Aid* %	*Total* %	*(No. of Cases)*
Local	77.1	22.9	100.0	(130)*
Non-local	34.9	65.1	100.0	(43)**

*Excludes 30 cases in which unmarried father's involvement was not sought by agency (control cases).

**Excludes 22 cases in which unmarried father's involvement was not sought by agency (control cases).

The figures in Table 15 strongly suggest that the unmarried father can be motivated to seek agency help, or that he will accept such help, when the unmarried mother encourages this agency relationship. When, on the other hand, she chooses to exclude him or exhibits no interest in having him involved, the unmarried father is, perforce,

Table 15. *Relationship Between Unmarried Mother's Active Assistance in Effecting Unmarried Father's Involvement and Agency's Success in Reaching the Unmarried Father*

Success in Reaching Unmarried Father When Unmarried Mother Participated	*Reached* %	*(No. of Cases)***
Unmarried fathers reached*	94.3	(109)
Unmarried fathers not reached	12.1	(116)

*Includes 13 unmarried fathers reached by letter and phone only.

**Excludes one case with no answer.

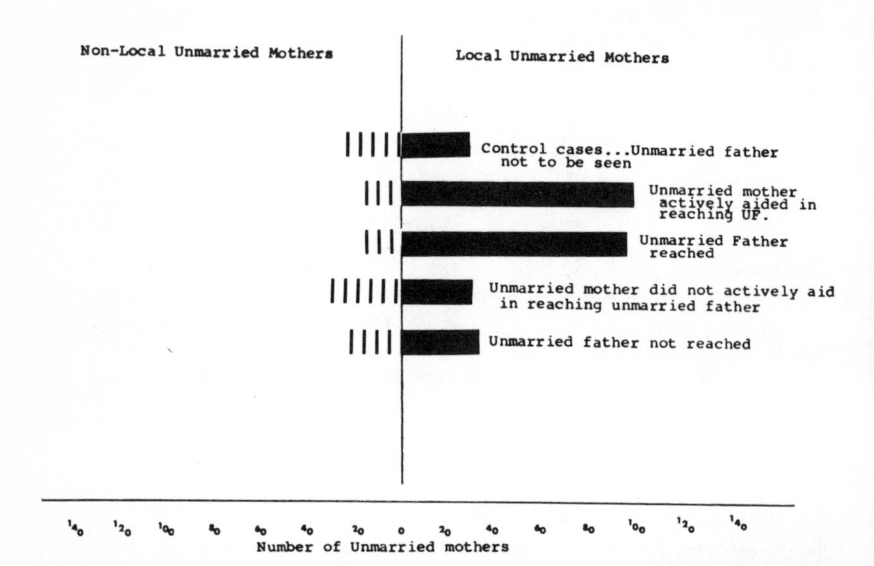

FIGURE 2. *Distribution of Frequency with which Unmarried Mothers Aided in Reaching Unmarried Fathers and Success in Reaching Unmarried Father by Residence (Local and Non-Local)*

less accessible and/or disinclined to respond to attempts to draw him into the social work program.

APPROACHES FOR REACHING THE UNMARRIED FATHER

Initial efforts by the caseworker to encourage the unmarried mother to name the unmarried father include telling her that the agency wishes to see him and urging her to get him to make an appointment. Early in the agency's contact with the mother, she is introduced to the male worker who has been assigned to the unmarried father. This allays some of her anxiety and makes it easier for her to explain to the father why the agency wishes to talk with him. If the father does not respond to this approach, the caseworker attempts to reach him by telephone and, if he is successful in doing so, he stresses any or all of the following points:

1. The agency the worker represents is not a legal agency or any arm of the law, but a *social* agency.
2. The worker does not have any preconceived ideas regarding solutions for the father's predicament, but will assist in exploring all alternatives.
3. The unmarried father's predicament requires help that the agency with its body of knowledge and experience can provide.
4. An out-of-wedlock pregnancy is serious and carries long-range implications for the unmarried father, the child, and the unmarried mother.
5. The importance of the unmarried father's emotional support of the unmarried mother (who is already coming to the agency for help) is stressed.
6. Legal implications, such as statutory rape, etc., *may* have to be explained, at the worker's discretion, to impress upon the unmarried father the importance of his becoming involved with the agency.

These points demonstrate that the agency energetically seeks out the unmarried father in what has been termed an assertive approach. Assertiveness, however, does not imply hostile, authoritarian, demanding attitudes. Rather, it implies a positive, firm stand based on the notion that the father's participation is important if the problem is to be tackled thoughtfully and effectively. The role of directness and candidness in this context is reaffirmed by the Family Centered Project of St. Paul, Minnesota:

> Progress has come through the steady discipline of holding ourselves to pointed as well as warm relationships with our clients and noting how much better people respond to clarity. We are no longer afraid to tell parents the dangers we see. We no longer need to gloss over reality. But we have never confused honesty with hostility.[1]

In the study reported here, efforts to establish involvement of the unmarried father with the agency required the worker to have a repertoire of skills and methods of approach, including various motivational approaches and appeals. Workers voiced the expectation that the unmarried father would participate and the belief that he *should.* They took a positive stand with the unmarried father's parents to this effect, and, when necessary, pointed out potential legal consequences that could result if the unmarried father failed to participate. The latter eventuality was not presented as a punitive measure, but rather as a reflection of prevailing, realistic social circumstances when —and only when—such circumstances did, in fact, exist, Much of the casework technique focused on assisting clients to separate fantasy from reality.

In addition to these direct approaches, workers also utilized motivations associated with human values. For example, caseworkers explored anxieties, questions, problems, plans for the future, and many other complex issues with the unmarried fathers as a way of pointing out the seriousness of the problem and the importance of continuing contact with a social agency.

An examination of the emotional appeals the workers directed to the fathers shows that slightly less attention was paid to assessing unmarried mother/unmarried father relationship problems, and to discussing personal growth in contact, when the unmarried father was over twenty-one than when he was younger. It may be that the unmarried father in the older age group was regarded as being more concerned with consequences and therefore as responding to motivations having to do with decision-making affecting plans for the baby and with his responsibility to the unmarried mother. As can be seen in Table 16, however, the differences in frequency of appeals directed to the two age categories were modest.

Merely reaching the unmarried father was not enough, of course. The purpose of having him come to the agency was to encourage him to explore his problem and to take an active part in making the decisions that would affect the future of all concerned. In general, once an unmarried father in this study was reached, and had visited the agency, he frequently expressed relief that someone was interested in his problem—that he could have a non-judgmental person to talk to about the implications of the predicament for the mother, the out-of-wedlock child, and himself.

One yardstick of his involvement was the extent of his participation in interviews with the caseworker (see Table 17).

Approximately two-thirds of the unmarried fathers included in the study took part in four or more casework interviews. Only 15 percent terminated their participation after one interview. While these figures do not necessarily measure the quality of the interaction, they do suggest that the unmarried father can indeed become significantly involved in casework with a social agency. It is equally evident, however, that the father's involvement, compared with that

TABLE 16. *Extent to Which Male Worker Used* Particular Motivational Appeals to Bring About the Unmarried Father's Involvement, by Age Category*

Motivation	*Frequency Motivation Was Used* Under 21 %	Over 21 %
Unmarried father's responsibility for child's welfare	56.9 (33)**	69.6 (25)
Unmarried father's responsibility for partner	56.9 (33)	66.6 (24)
Unmarried father's responsibility to see unmarried mother through difficult situation	77.6 (45)	75.0 (27)
Meaning of the situation to the unmarried father personally	58.6 (34)	41.7 (15)
Unmarried father's importance in decision-making (chiefly about plans for the baby)	77.6 (45)	83.3 (30)
Unmarried father's importance in assessing his relationship with unmarried mother	62.1 (36)	55.5 (20)

*An appeal was considered as used if worker marked his check-list either "to some degree" or "to a strong degree." More than one appeal may be used by worker.

**Figures in parentheses are numbers of cases.

TABLE 17. *Unmarried Parents' Interviews with Agency Caseworkers*

No. of Interviews	*Unmarried Fathers* %	*Unmarried Mothers* %
1 to 3	30.2*	16.3
4 to 7	34.4	20.8
8 to 12	27.1	27.0
13 to 17	8.3	18.6
18 or more	0.0	17.3
Total	100.0	100.0
(No. of cases)	(96)	(222)

*15% terminated after one interview.

of the unmarried mother, can be expected to be less extensive.

In short-term contacts of one to three interviews, opportunities to probe underlying problems are obviously fewer than when the client's association with the agency is of longer duration. As one might suspect, a short-term contact with an unmarried father necessitates focusing on readily identifiable and realistic goals of a relatively concrete nature. Even a single interview *can* have extreme significance, particularly if it deals candidly with specific issues such as decision-making around the future of the mother and child and the extent of the unmarried father's responsibility.

Unmarried Fathers Reached

In the study design, provisions were made for attempting to reach some unmarried fathers, whereas others were to serve as a "control group" and were not to be reached.[2] Furthermore, advance projections were made in regard to the number of unmarried fathers that would be reached in both categories. The projections and the percentages of unmarried fathers that were actually reached and not reached are shown in Table 18.

From the above table it can be seen that somewhat fewer unmarried fathers to be seen *were* seen than projected. In recalling the criteria that governed the establishment of the projected figures, it was noted that no provisions had been made for unmarried fathers not seen because of geographical constraints. The unmarried father located in a community far removed from the agency was not a

Table 18. *Projection of Success and Actual Success in Reaching Unmarried Fathers*

	Fathers to Be Seen		*Fathers Not to Be Seen*	
	Projected %	*Actual* %	*Projected* %	*Actual* %
Seen	67	50	30	26
Not seen	33	50	70	74
Total	100	100	100	100
(No. of cases)	(134)	(153)	(66)	(73)
	(X^2 4.65, df = 1; $p < .05$; significant)		(X^2 0.56, df = 1; $p < .90$; not significant)	

feasible subject for casework and study, a factor which was not weighed sufficiently in the design projections.[3]

Unmarried fathers actually seen who were *not* to have been seen were somewhat fewer than projected. This finding suggests that the casework staff incorporated into their thinking the concept of controlled experiment and that they exerted professional disciplined control in selecting cases for exception.[4]

Eliminating unmarried fathers who could not be seen by reason of geographic location, and eliminating those not seen by research design (control cases), our success in reaching unmarried fathers who were in the immediate area, and therefore realistically reachable, is shown in Table 19.

Nearly 80 percent of the fathers were in fact reached. Thus, it may be assumed that a high proportion of unmarried fathers *can* be seen through assertive casework methods when they reside within relatively adequate geographic access to the agency. This does not preclude, however, future experimentation with joint relationships among distant agencies that may, through careful training and

TABLE 19. *Percentages of Unmarried Fathers Living in the Community Who Were Seen and Were Not Seen (Experimental and Control Exception)*

	%
Total proportion of unmarried fathers seen	78.0
Total proportion of unmarried fathers to be seen who were not seen	22.0
Total	100.0
(No. of cases)	(123)

coordination of all participating staffs, extend the method to a broad geographic area.

Notes and References

1. *Casework Notebook.* St. Paul, Minn.: Minnesota Family Centered Project, Greater St. Paul Community Chest and Councils, 1957, p. 158.
2. The concepts of "experimental" and "control" groups are well stated in popular terms in Herbert Hyman's *Survey Design and Analysis.* (New York: The Free Press, 1966.) The intent here is, of course, to determine whether involvement of the unmarried father makes a difference to the mother, to the child, and to himself. These differences are considered in Chapter VI. Because of occasionally compelling casework considerations, the advance study design permitted rigidly limited opportunities for "fathers *not* to be seen" to be, in fact, seen.

   This relatively small group is noted in the extreme right-hand column of Table 18. See also Reuben Pannor and Byron W. Evans, "The Unmarried Father: Demonstration and Evaluation of an Assertive Casework Approach," in *Illegitimacy: Data and Findings for Prevention, Treatment and Policy Formulation.* New York: National Council on Illegitimacy, 1965, p. 55.
3. Attempts to reach the non-local unmarried fathers were made, using a variety of procedures, but limited time, staff, and money made this impractical. We explored the possibility of asking agencies in other communities to interview the unmarried father and, at the same time, to gather data comparable to the data we were gathering in our study. Because many agencies were not familiar with our methods, we discarded this plan. We dis-

cussed sending project staff into other communities to interview unmarried fathers, but this too proved impractical except for nearby communities. Correspondence was initiated with many out-of-state unmarried fathers, some of whom responded but, in general, gathering data through correspondence did not prove fruitful.

4. The following criteria for making exceptions to the control group and the method for effecting such changes were established in the interest of systematic procedure: 1) when the unmarried mother specifically initiated a request to contact the unmarried father; 2) when unmarried fathers presented themselves voluntarily and requested service; 3) when the referring agency specifically referred to the need to interview the unmarried father and indicated this had been discussed with the potential applicant; and 4) when unusual case situations arose which, in the worker's judgment, indicated that the adjustment of the mother or welfare of the child required contact with the unmarried father. If the caseworker decided to reach an unmarried father who was in the control group, such decision was discussed with the co-director at the agency, and if exception was to be made, discussion was held with the research associate prior to initiating any action.

V Sexual Ideology and the Sexual Act

The wave of change that is affecting our sexual mores is a favorite topic of current social commentary. In recent years, research projects have dealt with the frequency of sexual intercourse, with conditions affecting the occurrence of the act, and with physiological aspects of the act itself. Much less attention has been given to the personal meaning of the particular sexual event, especially if this event results in illegitimate pregnancy. In this chapter, we shall consider the psychological world of the unmarried parents who were the subjects of the study reported in this book.

Two opposing stereotypes are widely held. The first, and perhaps the most common of these, is the well-worn notion that the male partner proceeds without care, scattering his seed here and there, paying no attention to choice of partners and attaching no significance to the relationship. The second is the assumption that the premarital sex act is inevitably followed by severe personal regret, self-reproach and debilitation, for the man as well as for the woman. As matters turn out, the picture is more complicated than either of these threadbare views would indicate.

Social critics have suggested that in the "Sexy Sixties" and the "Sensate Seventies" anything was and is permissible and "good" as long as it is fun. This "fun morality" has little to say about responsibility, and neither is it tied to any firm tradition of timeless "rights and wrongs." Whether or not "moral" in the absolute sense, the findings in this study show that the majority of unmarried fathers, and a large group of unmarried mothers, did, indeed, feel that sexual intercourse was fun! (See Table 20.)

Approximately 28 percent of the unmarried fathers and 20 percent of the mothers viewed the sex act as unreservedly fun, with 35 percent and 50 percent, respectively, viewing the experience as not fun. True to one aspect of the popular image, the unmarried fathers seemed somewhat more carefree about the matter than the unmarried mothers. Fifty-one percent of the men agreed that the sex act was fun, as compared to 50 percent of the unmarried mothers. On the other hand, one-half of the unmarried mothers but only a bit more than one-third of the unmarried fathers decided that it was not fun at all. Thus, the female did emerge as a somewhat skeptical partner concerning the joys of the

TABLE 20. *Extent to Which Unmarried Parents Viewed Sex as "Fun"*

Degree of Fun	*Unmarried Fathers* %	*Unmarried Mothers* %
Fun	28.2	20.2
Fun–with reservations	22.3	26.2
Enjoyable–not fun	8.2	3.8
Exciting with one you care for	5.8	–
Not fun	35.3	50.0
Total	100.0*	100.0
(No. of cases)	(85)	(156)

*Rounded to 100.0%.

act, but the difference was not dramatic. However, the idea of having a good time, without explicit concern for consequences, was prevalent among both sexes.

What about guilt? It appeared to be of some significance, particularly with the unmarried fathers, but not nearly to the degree that might be expected on the basis of the common stereotype. Only about one unmarried father in eight admitted to some feelings of guilt. (The corresponding figure for the unmarried mothers was much lower.) From their vantage point, caseworkers detected the presence of guilt in much greater proportion and more often among the unmarried fathers than among the unmarried mothers—60 percent versus 50 percent (Table 21).

It appears, then, that guilt is not entirely an issue of the past and that the beacon of fun does not illuminate the sexual labyrinth without also casting a dimming after-shadow. Rather, guilt and fun emerge as uneasy partners. Fun

TABLE 21. *Guilt Feelings of Unmarried Parents as Perceived by Caseworkers*

Worker Perception	*Unmarried Fathers** %	*Unmarried Mothers*** %
Guilt feelings perceived	60.2	50.3
No guilt feelings perceived	39.8	49.7
Total	100.0	100.0
(No. of cases)	(93)	(193)

(X^2 4.55, df = 1; $p < .05$)

*Excludes 2 cases in which attitudes were not assessed.
**Excludes 28 cases in which attitudes were not assessed.

predominates, by far. But guilt does enter the picture, probably in greater measure than the sexual partners, especially the unmarried fathers, are ready to admit (see Table 22).

Parents spend considerable effort and emotional energy in urging their children to guide their sex life in some specific direction, often a direction defined by firm religious or ethical structures. They may disapprove of intercourse outside marriage, hoping thereby to set standards that will preserve hallowed values and prevent rash actions—including those that result in pregnancy. Few of the unmarried mothers or fathers in this study appeared to be influenced by parental admonition. Only 2 percent of the fathers and 1 percent of the mothers reported feeling any concern about parental disapproval. Either conventional constraints were used little by the parents or, more probably, the admonition of "don't" simply proved ineffective, at least at a conscious level.

The following list of items, although long and varied, suggests that unmarried parents are perhaps overly concerned with meeting their own immediate needs. Consideration of the partner or of the consequences of the sexual act was conspicuous by its infrequency. Fear of pregnancy was cited as a factor of concern twice by unmarried fathers and six times by unmarried mothers. Concern for parental disapproval appears four times for unmarried fathers and three times for unmarried mothers. In no instance does concern for consequences to partner appear as an important consideration.

For some, the taste of combat flavored the relationship. It was the female who appeared as the predator. While the process of expressing hostility was subtle, and while numbers do not tell the full story, it seems that one unmarried father in twelve noted that the unmarried mother was the aggressor. Only a very small proportion of mothers con-

TABLE 22. *Meanings Unmarried Parents Associate with the Sex Act*

	Unmarried Fathers %	*Unmarried Mothers* %
Need to be loved and cared for	3.0	5.6
Potential way of getting married	4.0	4.0
To please unmarried mother/unmarried father	3.0	9.2
Fully expected to marry partner	0.5	2.0
Saw experience as something that was expected of them	3.4	3.3
To meet dependency needs	4.5	3.0
To prove masculinity/femininity	4.5	4.0
To create image of sophistication	1.1	1.0
Fear of discovery	5.6	1.6
Feelings of guilt	13.1	5.3
Hostile feelings toward partner	8.5	6.6
Experience too brief	5.1	0.6
Breaking up of relationship following act	3.4	4.6
Setting inappropriate	7.4	4.0

	Unmarried Fathers %	*Unmarried Mothers* %
Depression following act	3.4	2.6
Self-punitive	1.1	5.0
Lack of self-esteem, self-confidence	7.4	9.2
Concern with parental disapproval	2.2	1.0
Wasn't worth it	1.7	1.3
Under influence of alcohol	1.1	1.0
Tired of resisting advances	1.1	0.6
Defiance	3.0	1.3
Unmarried mother the aggressor	8.5	1.6
Unmarried father the aggressor	2.2	2.6
Fear of pregnancy	1.1	2.0
Way of holding unmarried father	–	7.5
Desire to have baby	–	5.0
Tricked/attacked	–	3.6
Way of gaining identity	–	2.6
Total	100.0*	100.0*
(No. of responses)	(176)	(303)

*Because categories are not mutually exclusive, total number of qualities may exceed number of subjects.

sidered themselves in this role, but some (5 percent) believed that the sex act was, in some way, an act of *self*-punishment. This is further supported by the finding that 10 percent of the unwed mothers admitted to a lack of self-esteem and to doubts about their own worthiness. Perhaps to smite the serpent of self-doubt, one mother in ten regarded the sex act as a means of pleasing her partner, and had no concern for her own well-being; and one in 13 invited the act as a way to hold the father. The once prevalent view that the male somehow "tricks" the female into a relationship which he then exploits, was not widely shared, even among the unmarried mothers.

The high percentage of unmarried parents (mothers, approximately 74 percent and fathers, approximately 79 percent) who viewed pregnancy as something that "just happened" reinforced the concept that unmarried parents failed to relate the sexual act to possible consequences (see Table 23).

Isolation of acts from consequences suggests an orientation with the present, as opposed to planned behavior affecting the future. Caseworkers were asked to indicate the extent to which the unmarried mother/unmarried father dealt with the present—with the "here-and-now." They reported that they perceived 75 percent of the unmarried fathers and 64 percent of the unmarried mothers as dealing with the here-and-now rather than with future consequences.

This study was carried on largely in the era before the popularity of the "pill." Therefore, knowledge of conventional means of contraception was a significant factor. One thing was immediately clear: the pregnancies did not result simply because of a lack of *knowledge* about contraception. Practically all of the unmarried mothers, and the fathers too, knew something about it though we may, of course, question the sophistication of their knowledge or their skills

Table 23. *Extent to Which Unmarried Parents Regarded Pregnancy as Something That "Just Happened," as Perceived by Workers*

	*Unmarried Fathers** %	*Unmarried Mothers*** %
Attitude perceived by caseworker	79.1	73.7
Attitude not perceived by caseworker	20.9	26.3
Total	100.0	100.0
(No. of cases)	(91)	(179)
(X^2 0.37, df = 1; p > .50, not significant)		

*Excludes 2 cases in which attitude was not assessed.
**Excludes 21 cases in which attitude was not assessed.

in the use of contraceptives. Further, the vast majority did not feel that difficulty in *obtaining* contraceptives was a factor in limiting their use (see Tables 24 and 25).

Although a somewhat greater proportion of unmarried mothers than unmarried fathers viewed obtaining contraceptives as a problem, differences were not statistically significant. Furthermore, taken as a group, only one-fifth of the unmarried parents saw blocks, real or imagined, in the way of obtaining contraceptives.

Then there is the matter of prior *experience* with contraceptives. About one-half of the unmarried mothers and unmarried fathers—suprisingly equal proportions—had employed contraceptives on a previous occasion. The pregnancies, therefore, could not be blamed on lack of informa-

TABLE 24. *Extent to Which Unmarried Parents Knew About Contraceptives*

Knew About Contraceptives	*Unmarried Fathers* %	*Unmarried Mothers* %
Yes	100.0	98.1
No	0.0	1.9
Total	100.0	100.0
(No. of cases)	(73)	(156)

(X^2 not computable because expected frequencies less than 5 in two cells)

TABLE 25. *Extent to Which Unmarried Mothers and Unmarried Fathers Felt That Obtaining Contraceptives Was a Problem*

Obtaining Contraceptives Was a Problem	*Unmarried Fathers* %	*Unmarried Mothers* %
Yes	15.5	23.1
No	84.5	76.9
Total	100.0	100.0
(No. of cases)	(58)	(108)

(X^2 1.42, $df = 1$; $p < .30$; not significant)

tion, or on lack of experience with means of preventing conception. What then, seems to be the reason for the non-use of contraceptives?

Some of the answers were supplied by the unmarried fathers themselves. Nearly half said simply that they didn't like contraceptives. Another 24 percent indicated that the act had not been planned, while 12 percent had acted on faith—they just felt that nothing would happen.

In summary, the emerging pattern, as far as attitudes toward the sex act are concerned, is one of lack of concern for consequences and an emphasis on fun, intermingled occasionally with guilt or hostility. Simple exploitation or trickery occurs rarely, all the folklore on this topic notwithstanding.

Black Star, Werner Wolff

The Unmarried Father: From Shadow to Reality: Part II

Don sat in the waiting room of the agency, feeling isolated and anxious at the thought of the interview to come. There were several other people in the waiting room, but he was numbly indifferent to their presence, his feelings focused entirely inward. His sense of isolation, even of alienation, was the thing he had found hardest to bear over the past week. It was as though he had suddenly been cut off, hung in mid-air, denied meaningful human contact. He couldn't discuss his feelings with his mother, his father, or even with Betty. How then could he talk about them with a stranger? If, at that moment, he could have conceived of any safe place to hide, he would have gone there.

"Don? I'm Mr. West."

He looked up and saw a man with a pleasant noncommittal expression on his face gazing down at him—an ordinary man, probably about his father's age. His hand was out, so Don rose awkwardly and shook hands.

"Come with me. My office is down this hall."

Don followed Mr. West without speaking. He was shown into a small office containing a desk and chair, bookshelves, and two easy chairs. Don sat down in one of the chairs as Mr. West sat behind his desk. Don cleared his throat nervously and pretended to study the titles of the books on the shelves, just so he could put his eyes somewhere, on something, besides Mr. West. He wished he felt sure enough of himself to light a cigarette, but he knew that if he tried, his hands would shake.

Mr. West rearranged some papers on his desk, and began to talk easily and casually. "The first thing I want you to know, Don, is that I am not here to make any moral judgments. I'm not, in any sense, an enforcer of the law. I want to try to help you understand the situation you're in, and to indicate possible solutions to some of the problems confronting you. After you and I have discussed the problems, I'll talk to your parents and, hopefully, among all of us, we can arrive at some solutions."

Don nodded, and relaxed a little in his chair. He had had a vague idea that he was there to be judged, tried, and sentenced, and the knowledge that this was not so relieved at least some of his tension. But as Mr. West began to discuss the situation in detail, Don saw that, although he might not be there to be judged, he was there to examine the reality of the situation confronting him, which, in his state of emotional turmoil, he hadn't yet really begun to do. And the reality of the situation was not pleasant.

Mr. West pointed out that Betty's parents, if they wanted to, could file rape charges against him. In addition, he was liable to being placed on probation for at least a year. But more important than either of these possibilities, Don must force himself to face the fact that a baby was going to be born, a living human being whom Don had helped create. Plans would have to be made for that infant's existence after birth, and Don should assume a responsible role in whatever plans were to be made.

It was the first time that Don had really believed in the existence of a child or thought of himself as a father. The thing that made it seem most real was remembering his two-year-old brother at home, who was still a baby. The fact that he, Don, could be the father of such a child was overwhelming. He had some idea of the responsibilities involved in raising a child but, truthfully, he could not see himself fulfilling them.

Mr. West told Don that it was inevitable that he should experience a sense of panic and inadequacy in confronting the problem, and that perhaps it would be of most benefit if Don could be helped to understand how the situation had evolved. Betty would be receiving similar counseling, and after each of them had gained some perspective, they would, maybe, be able to help each other.

Don agreed, and in subsequent interviews he found he was able, with some degree of objectivity, to discuss himself, his relations with his family, his self-image, and perhaps most important of all because it bothered him most, his fear of sexual inadequacy.

He described himself as being often moody. He said that while he made friends quite easily, the friendships were usually on a superficial level. He was a good student. He enjoyed most of the school social functions, but didn't participate in any extracurricular activities.

His relations with his family were a source of anxiety to him. His feelings toward his mother were conflicting ones—he felt very close to her, he knew he could rely on her for comfort, but he could not bring himself to discuss his experiences and problems with her. She was always there to talk to; in fact, she was "there" too much—he had the feeling that she hovered over him—picking up his clothes, straightening his room, fixing special food—and he often wished she would focus more of her attention on his father, and less on him. At the same time, he wished she were sometimes there on a level that would permit real communication.

His feelings toward his father were ambivalent, too. He admired his father, but he resented his always being too busy to talk to him, his superficial air of man-to-man camaraderie, his casualness toward Don as a son. He felt that as far as his father was concerned, he might just as well be "the kid next door," so basically impersonal was their relationship. He didn't like the way his father treated his mother—downgrading her as a homemaker, arguing with her about money, and accusing her of being too old and uncaring.

When he met Betty, he felt that at last he had found someone to whom he was genuinely important on all levels—intellectually, emotionally, and physically. She was just fifteen, but she responded to him in ways that he needed—she listened to him, she responded physically to him; he felt that she cared about him, sensed that she needed him in almost the same way that he needed her, and when they decided to go steady, it gave him a sense of security, a sense of closeness to another person that he had not had before.

He and Betty were at a drive-in movie the night they first had sex. The movie was filled with sex; there seemed to be bodies all over the screen. He and Betty had been engaged in heavy necking—it wasn't the first time they had done that—and this time Betty's resistance was so weak that Don easily persuaded her to make love. It was an awkward, clumsy experience that lasted only a few minutes, and it left both of them feeling "separate" and unsatisfied. Don felt ashamed and guilty about it, and the next day he found it hard to talk to Betty. Yet they continued to go together and to have sexual intercourse.

Don revealed that he had had one sexual experience with a girl before Betty—a girl who was more sexually experienced than he—and he "hadn't made it." The experience was so ego shattering that he hadn't even tried to see the girl again. When he did "make it" with Betty, the fact that the experience wasn't satisfying to him (and he didn't think it was to her, either) disturbed him deeply. Having sex was supposed to be one of life's great experiences, according to the books and magazines he read and the movies and TV shows he watched, but for him it wasn't. Did that mean that he was lacking in some way? He supposed it must, because one of his friends, who'd been going steady for several months, had told him that he and his girl really had a good time having sex. Don knew the girl. She was a lot more—well, physical—than Betty. She was a couple of years older than Betty, and she was, well, she was really built, *and he wondered if that might have something to do with it. But he really didn't think so. Betty was always willing, when he wanted to, and a guy couldn't expect any more than that, could he?*

So he and Betty kept on having intercourse—usually in the back seat of his father's car——and it didn't get any better. They were always afraid someone would discover them. Betty was always withdrawn and uncommunicative afterwards; he really didn't know what she felt. It was the one thing they couldn't discuss. Each time they had sex, their whole relationship seemed to deteriorate; they both became mute and withdrawn, and would avoid seeing each other the next day.

Once, when her mother was at a meeting, they had gone to Betty's house and had sex in her parents' bed. They pretended they were married; she had made lunch, he'd helped with the dishes, and then they'd gone to bed. But it wasn't any more satisfying than their experiences in the car had been.

That was the only time they'd really planned to have sex. The rest of the time, they'd just ended up doing it. He initiated it each time more because he felt he was sup-

posed to than because he wanted to. He felt it was expected of him now.

When Mr. West asked Don if they had attempted to use contraceptives, Don revealed that his knowledge about them was fairly haphazard. He had heard of diaphragms, but he didn't know exactly what they were; he had never heard of the intrauterine devices. He knew about birth control pills, but he also knew that the girl had to see a doctor and get a prescription, and he couldn't see Betty doing that; he didn't even ask her to consider it. He did know what condoms were; in fact, he often carried one. But he felt embarrassed about having to buy them, and even more ill at ease using them. He'd used them twice with Betty—but it seemed so stupid to stop in the middle of everything and tell Betty to wait until he got it on and was ready. And the two times he did use them, Betty told him they bothered her.

He and Betty had talked about the use of contraceptives once. She thought it was his responsibility, and he felt it was hers. Don had the vague impression that when a boy is out with a girl he really cares for, like Betty, using contraceptives just isn't right; they should be used only with girls you don't care about. And neither he nor Betty ever talked or thought about the future.

Mr. West was able to make Don see that he and Betty had both lacked the assurance, the sophistication, the privacy, and the caring about the future that would have enabled them to use contraceptives effectively.

Don told Mr. West that he had been masturbating since he was fourteen. An acquaintance had told him that only homosexuals masturbate, and while he didn't really believe this, it bothered him because he knew that he got more pleasure from masturbating than from sex with Betty.

Mr. West explained that it was not unusual for boys

his age to masturbate; nor was it unusual for them to be disappointed in their relationships with girls. The secrecy and guilt that accompanied their relationships with girls, and their preoccupation with satisfying their personal needs only, prevented real gratification. A satisfactory sexual relationship only develops when people feel a mature commitment to one another. It develops when there is a minimum of guilt. A boy and girl in the back seat of a car are not free from guilt, or fear of discovery, or ready for the emotional commitment that most satisfying sexual relationships require.

Don learned that Betty had been subject to stresses and anxieties not too different from his own, which was one reason their relationship had developed and disintegrated in the way it had. They both possessed tremendous needs which they had attempted to fulfill through each other, and which neither of them was capable of fulfilling for the other.

Betty's relationship with her father had always been remote. Her mother, in an attempt to escape from her maternal role, which had never satisfied her, had given Betty too much freedom, letting her do whatever she wanted in order to avoid arguments. And Betty had reacted with anger, demanding more and more freedom, when she instinctively sensed she already had too much. Betty was submissive with Don, essentially because she needed to be submissive with someone. She too, was unhappy and disappointed with their sexual relationship, but couldn't bring herself to tell Don how she felt. She had continued to have sex with him because she believed it pleased him.

That their sexual relationship, which had been so unsatisfying to both of them, should have resulted in a baby seemed to Don ironic and unjust. But he had begun to realize that while Betty's pregnancy perhaps marked the end of what had seemed to be his most significant relation-

ship with another human being, it also marked the beginning of something else—a confrontation with himself, and with reality.

Betty was confronting reality, too. In the beginning of her pregnancy, she had considered the possibility of marrying Don. It would have been, in the eyes of many people she knew, the "respectable" thing to do. And she had conjured up, at first, a fairly romantic picture of housekeeping. But the realities of their youth, their immaturity, their inexperience, Don's meagre earning capacity, her own ineptness—she didn't really know anything about babies or keeping house—were too overwhelming. She and Don, with counseling, with support from both their families, had been able to discuss their predicament with each other without too much strain. But the more time passed, the more they talked, the more she realized how unready they both were for marriage. She had been infatuated with him, and he with her, but their infatuation had been based on weakness, not strength, and that was no foundation for a marriage.

She also considered, briefly, the possibility of keeping the baby herself, and raising it with her mother's help. Her parents told her they would stand by her in whatever decision she made, but that should she decide to keep the baby, she would have to assume the major responsibility of caring for it. And she had grown too increasingly aware of her own faults, and her mother's weaknesses as a parent, to believe that they could, even together, even trying hard, give a child the emotional sustenance and security it would need.

Thus, when the baby was born—a normal, healthy, seven-pound baby girl—Betty and Don, together, decided to place the baby for adoption. But, although they had ex-

plored and rejected the alternatives, giving up the baby was not easy for either of them.

Betty was able to see the infant for several days after she was born, and she derived pride and delight from holding her, feeding her, and caring for her. She named her Donna, after Don, even though she knew the adoptive parents would rename her.

Don also saw the baby—at the social agency. Arrangements were made for the baby to be brought there for that purpose. Even with his developing self-awareness, Don had not realized the depth of emotion he would feel for his infant daughter. He was proud, and he was afraid, and when, as he held the baby, she began to cry and he didn't know what to do, he realized clearly—and not without a sense of loss—that he could not give his child what she most needed from him—the strength of a father.

Betty was the only one required to sign the relinquishment papers that gave the baby up for adoption, but Don was a witness to the relinquishment.

He left the agency, as he had come, alone. He no longer felt angry or fearful or alienated. He had helped decide the future of his child, and he knew the decision that had been reached was the best one. But he ached with sadness, and he knew, because he was beginning to know himself, that that ache might be with him the rest of his life.

VI Making the Decision: The Fate of the Child

The decisions made by the unwed parents and their families before the mother gives birth not only affect the child, but the parents as well. Various alternatives for the child's future must be explored within a relatively short period of time. The often painful implications of whatever decisions are made must be examined thoroughly if a sound new beginning is to be provided for all concerned.

Several alternatives are available to the unwed parents: 1) they may seek an abortion*; 2) they may marry and keep the child; 3) the mother may keep the baby and rear it by herself; 4) the mother may keep the baby and rear it within a larger family unit, most often with *her* mother assuming major responsibility; 5) the mother may place the child in a foster home where the major responsibility of raising the child is carried by the foster parents; 6) the father may make the plans and either have *his* parents care for the child or place it in a foster home; or 7) the child may be placed for adoption. Exploration of these alternatives can best be accomplished by bringing together those vitally involved in the matter—the unwed mother, the unwed father, and especially in the case of teen-agers, their parents.

Comparatively little attention has been given to the

*Changes in the law in some states in 1969 and 1970 liberalizing the circumstances under which abortions may be obtained now make legal abortions a more meaningful alternative.

process of decision-making relating to plans for the baby. Even less attention has been given to the impact of the unmarried father on the decision-making process. To assume that the unmarried mother should arrive at decisions about the baby without consideration of its father is, in effect, denying his very existence or denying the fact that a meaningful relationship has ever existed between the mother and father. It is only in relatively rare instances, when the relationship has indeed been so casual that neither unwed parent really knew much about the other, that such an assumption is valid. Our studies have shown that the relationships between unwed mothers and unwed fathers are much more meaningful than popularly supposed, and that unwed fathers have more concern for their offspring than is generally realized.

As noted in Chapter I, a common image of the unwed father is that of a man who gives only fleeting attention, if any, to the problems resulting from out-of-wedlock conception and birth and who, more likely, seeks to ignore (or evade) further involvement altogether. He thereby becomes the "forgettable" or "forgotten" man and is—perhaps too conveniently—excluded from participation in making decisions regarding the child. However, it is our belief that indeed the father *has* a responsibility, not only to participate in planning for the child's future, but also to examine the personal and social implications of his actions, as these affect the unwed mother, himself and—most importantly—the child's destiny. Exploration of alternatives that do not include the unwed father are, at best, halfway approaches to the solution of these problems.

The essence of an agency's or an individual's work with the unwed mother and father before the birth of their baby is assistance in the decision-making process, and help in relating what is happening in the present to what happened in the relevant past so that these experiences can be used to establish a basis for potential personal growth. The essence of work done with unwed parents after the birth of their baby is to help them to live with the decisions they have made.

In our study, we were particularly interested in knowing what effect the father's being involved had upon decisions made by the unmarried mother. To provide a measure for this, one group of unmarried fathers received counseling while another group were purposely *not* counseled by the agency. It is noteworthy that the decisions as such made by the unmarried mother regarding the future of the baby were not significantly affected by involvement of the father in casework counseling. In approximately 92 percent of the cases where the unmarried father was seen, the casework goal of helping the unmarried mother to arrive at an appropriate decision with respect to the baby's future was realized. Similarly, for 94 percent of the cases where the unmarried father was not seen, this goal was attained (see Table 26).

Once the unmarried mother had made her decision, it seemed relatively fixed, and little change occurred during the counseling period. Furthermore, this pattern was not altered by involvement of the unmarried father.

In instances in which the unmarried father was seen, 42.2 percent of the unmarried mothers who came to the agency planned to keep their babies. The final decision to keep was made by 36.8 percent, a difference of only 5.4 percent. Similarly, in instances in which the unmarried mother initially expressed the decision to place the child for adoption, the decision did not change appreciably over the period of time during which the unmarried mother was counseled.

For the sample in which the unmarried father was not

TABLE 26. *Extent to Which the Goal of Helping the Unmarried Mother Make the Appropriate Decision with Respect to the Baby's Future Was Reached for Experimental and Control Groups*

Attainment of Goal	*Experimental (Father Seen)* %	*Control (Father Not Seen)* %	*Total* %
Attained	92.4	93.8	92.9
Not attained	7.6	6.2	7.1
Total	100.0	100.0	100.0
(No. of cases)	(64)	(47)	(113)

(X^2 not computable)

seen 13.5 percent of the unmarried mothers who came to the agency planned to keep their babies. The final decision to keep was made by 11.1 percent, a difference of 2.4 percent. Little change occurred for those who had originally decided to place the baby for adoption.

Tables 27 and 28 show that unmarried mothers who came to the agency brought with them predetermined decisions regarding the baby, decisions that had been influenced by the constraints of the solutions that were realistically available to them. These decisions were not altered appreciably by intervention on the part of the caseworkers or significantly affected by involvement of the unmarried father. For instance, a Caucasian teen-aged unmarried mother, attending high school, dependent financially and emotionally upon her parents, lacking readiness for marriage, and facing the unwillingness of her parents to

TABLE 27. *Extent to Which Unmarried Mothers Kept Their Babies as Compared with Expressed Desire to Keep Early in Casework—Father Seen*

Attitude Before Birth of Child	%	*Action After Birth of Child*	%
Desire to keep	42.2	Kept	36.8
Desire not to keep	57.8	Not kept	63.2
Total	100.0		100.0
(No. of cases)	(71)		(68)

(X^2 0.48, df = 1; $p > .30$, not significant)

TABLE 28. *Extent to Which Unmarried Mothers Kept Their Babies as Compared with Expressed Desire to Keep Early in Casework—Father Not Seen*

Attitude Before Birth of Child	%	*Action After Birth of Child*	%
Desire to keep	13.5	Kept	11.1
Desire not to keep	86.5	Not Kept	88.9
Total	100.0		100.0
(No. of cases)	(52)		(45)

(X^2 .034, df = 1; $p > .80$, not significant)

allow her to bring the baby home, was left with adoption as the only feasible course of action. On the other hand, a Negro unmarried mother may have been able to consider only the alternative of keeping the child because adoptive homes were not available; and a non-local unmarried mother, planning to return to her home community, may have seen only one alternative as feasible—that of adoption.

It becomes evident that *apparent* alternative solutions often are not realistic alternatives. One must, therefore, come to grips with the fact that what appears to be a series of choices is not truly that when viewed in the context of each individual life situation and social milieu. Extension of social services to all unmarried mothers regardless of economic circumstances, racial or religious background, and the availability of more adoptive homes—these and other steps can help to provide genuine, workable alternative choices.

Decisions Reached

In approximately 62 percent of the 226 cases studied, the unmarried mother placed the baby for adoption. In some 20 percent of the cases, babies were kept by the mothers, in either and out-of-wedlock status or in marriage (Table 29).

Table 29. *Actions Taken by Unmarried Mothers in Respect to Their Out-of-Wedlock Children*

Action Taken	%
Mother placed baby for adoption	62.4
Mother kept baby	19.9
Other*	11.9
Don't know**	5.8
Total	100.0
(No. of cases)	(226)

*Includes cases such as: baby not born at conclusion of project; decision pending; etc.

**Includes cases in which unmarried mother terminated agency contact prior to birth of baby.

The relationship of those who kept their babies to those who married, and the relationship of those who kept to whether or not the unmarried father was seen, appear in Table 30.

Effects of the Unmarried Father's Support of the Unmarried Mother on Her Decision

Whenever the unmarried father was willing to stand by the unmarried mother and to share responsibility for her predicament, this proved to be of considerable psychological help to her. Her fear of hostile desertion was frequently dispelled. She could see the father as a person who was not running away but who was concerned, perhaps even frightened—at any rate, willing to help. His support of the unmarried mother in her awesome decision regarding the baby was also significant. Our findings showed that

TABLE 30. *Mothers Who Kept, by Category of Married/Did Not Marry, and Unmarried Father Seen/Not Seen*

Marital Status of Mother	*Unmarried Father Seen* %	*Unmarried Father Not Seen* %	*Total* %
Married (UF or someone else)	33.3	13.3	25.6
Did not marry	66.6	86.7	73.3
Total	100.0*	100.0	100.0
(No. of cases)	(30)	(15)	(45)

*Rounded to 100.0%.

when the unmarried father was involved, and when he and the mother could be brought together to discuss what was best for the baby, the mother felt personally reassured and more confident that the final decision was right. Study results also indicated that when the father received agency counseling, he more often supported the mother by approving her decision regarding the baby (Table 31). Seventy-eight percent of the unmarried fathers seen by the agency approved the unmarried mother's decision and conveyed this approval to her.

Of the unmarried fathers seen, only 2 percent were unaware of the mother's final decision regarding the baby. On the other hand, 41 percent of the fathers not seen were unaware of the mother's final decision. One wonders what

TABLE 31. *Extent to Which Unmarried Fathers Approved of Unmarried Mother's Final Decision Concerning Plans for the Baby, by Category of Fathers Seen and Fathers Not Seen*

Extent of Approval	*Father Seen* %	*Father Not Seen* %	*Total* %
Approved	78.3	50.0	68.4
Disaproved	20.0	9.4	16.3
Unmarried father unaware of final decision	1.7	40.6	15.4
Total	100.0	100.0	100.0
(No. of cases)	(60)*	(32)**	(92)

(X^2 43.63, df = 2; $p < .001$, significant)

*Excludes 14 cases in which question not answered.
**Excludes 21 cases in which question not answered.

the effects of not knowing the decision as to the baby's future may have been on the fathers not seen. We do know, from experience, that unmarried fathers have greater concern for their offspring than was heretofore generally believed.

Having the support of the father takes on lasting meaning for the unmarried mother, particularly since she must live with the consequences of the decision in the context of the relationship that led to the child's conception and birth. In our study, direct contacts between the unmarried father and the caseworker provided an opportunity to determine the father's attitude and the nature of his relationship with the mother. These attitudes were, in turn, conveyed to the mother either by her social worker or by a direct meeting between the unwed parents. In this meeting, the unmarried father often made clear his feelings about the unmarried mother, what future direction they both might take, and his wishes as far as the baby was concerned.

The unmarried mother who regarded the father as a potential husband was either helped to reinforce this feeling and to move toward the possibility of marriage or, if marriage was not feasible, she was helped to discard the idea of marriage to him as unrealistic. Sometimes the unmarried mother professed that the father had an interest in her or the baby when this did not actually exist. In these cases confrontation, either directly or through the caseworker, helped to dispel this fantasy and place the situation in the proper context.

The caseworkers who counseled the unmarried fathers noted that the fathers' involvement became a potent force in strengthening and supporting the decisions affecting all concerned. It was noted that the unmarried fathers, in the course of their involvement, helped to clarify their attitudes toward mother and baby, thereby permitting a more genuine assessment of potentials for marriage, and of the relevant relationships. When the father's participation was minimal or lacking entirely, the mother was helped nonetheless to examine his strengths and weaknesses. This further helped to establish a sound basis for the decision that had to be made.

The Unmarried Father Gains from Participation in Decision-Making

Whenever possible, the unmarried father was encouraged to see the baby. Seeing and holding it helped him recognize more clearly and dramatically the significance of his actions—the bringing of a new life into the world. His reaction was often one of pride and personal concern expressed by such comments as: "Is this baby really mine?" "I can't believe that I'm the father of a baby." "Is the baby receiving good care?" At first, most fathers were afraid to touch their baby, although they did so when encouraged by the social worker. Many took delight in feeding the baby. But when the infant cried or needed to be changed, the father's reaction often changed dramatically from wonder or joy to a realization that the baby was indeed a human being with needs for nurturing and care that he was unprepared to meet.

Unmarried Father's Financial Contribution

One guiding principle in working with unmarried fathers was that they should be encouraged to behave responsibly toward the unmarried mother and the baby. To encourage responsible action in a concrete, easily understood manner, caseworkers often asked unmarried fathers to help pay the costs of medical and maternity care. Caseworkers assumed that they would have to raise the issue of financial contribution if this was to be forthcoming. In some instances, however, this was not necessary, as, for example, when the unmarried father volunteered to contribute, or when the worker's knowledge of the father's finances indicated that no monetary contribution should be expected or asked for.

Stress on actual or potential financial responsibility further emphasized the fact that, should the unmarried mother decide to keep the baby, it was possible that the father might later be held responsible for child support. This was not presented to the father as a threat, but rather as a realistic possibility, and as a way of helping him recognize that he had a vital stake in decisions that were made. In 59 percent of the cases, caseworkers suggested that the unmarried father should contribute financially (see Table 32).

TABLE 32. *Frequency with Which Male Caseworkers Raised the Issue of Financial Contribution by the Father*

Worker's Action	%
Raised issue	59.1
Did not raise issue*	30.1
Did not apply**	10.8
Total	100.0
(No. of cases)	(93)

*Cases in this category included unmarried fathers who volunteered to make financial contributions, and cases where action was contraindicated.

**Cases in this category included couples who married, cases where plans had already been made, etc.

Although the male worker may not have raised the issue directly in 40 percent of the cases, both he and the female worker did, in various ways, make the agency's expectations about this issue known to the unwed parents, and to *their* parents as well.

In a few instances, workers felt it necessary to enlist the active aid of others in their efforts to enunciate and clarify for the father the "responsibility" concept. Again, help was solicited from the parents of either or both of the unwed parents (see Table 33).

The extent to which the unmarried fathers contributed is shown in Figure 3. These represent only those amounts known to the agency. Funds were contributed in various ways. In some instances, payments were made to the agency for transmission to mother or hospital, and in others they were directly to the concerned parties, i.e., the hospital, the doctor, the unmarried mother herself, or the unmarried mother's parents. In all, 46 contributions were made by a total of 55 unmarried fathers for whom it had been determined that they were indeed financially able to contribute. They ranged in amount from $10 to $1,050 with a median of $237.50, thus were usually more than token amounts. Generally, the fathers followed through with whatever commitment they made.

TABLE 33. *Extent of Solicitation and Persons Solicited for Help in Expressing to Unmarried Fathers the Importance of Their Financial Participation*

Unmarried mother	6.4%
Unmarried father's parents	5.3%
Unmarried mother's parents	5.3%

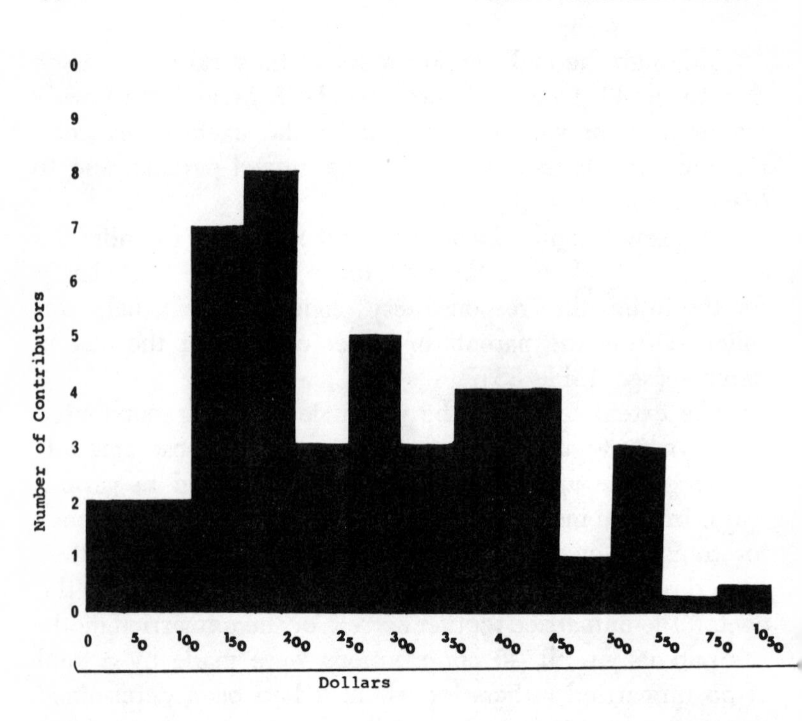

FIGURE 3. *Distribution of Contributions Made by Unmarried Fathers to Vista Del Mar for Meeting Maternity Costs Incurred by Unmarried Mothers*

Our experience in this study demonstrated that unmarried fathers *will* participate financially. Not only does this lighten the financial burden for the unwed mother's family or welfare agency, but it provides a concrete means whereby the unwed father assumes some responsibility for the outcome of his behavior.

VII Background and Personality of Unwed Parents

How do unwed parents differ from other parents? How do couples who conceive out of wedlock and marry when the pregnancy is discovered differ from those who likewise conceive out of wedlock but do not marry? (It has been estimated that one out of every five brides is carrying a child.) How do unmarried mothers who have abortions differ from those who bear their babies and then place them for adoption? And how about those who keep their out-of-wedlock children?

These are questions worth asking but, unfortunately, it is still impossible to answer them in detail. Identifying parents who marry after the woman has become pregnant, or mothers who seek abortions, poses an intricate and largely elusive research problem.

Although some data on characteristics of unmarried mothers have been available, there has been little information concerning the personalities of unmarried fathers. In this chapter, we shall consider some of the personality traits and characteristics of unwed parents, fathers included. Our conclusions about unmarried parents are derived from grouped data. The patterns obtained should not be regarded as stereotypes because there is, of course, a realistic range of individual differences among unwed parents. By characterizing groups, however, clues to personality configuration can be developed that establish a context for the assessment of individual problems.

Background

A brief review of the key factors in unwed parents' backgrounds may serve as a prelude to the description of their personality attributes.

Education

According to currently available data (1969), the education level of the unmarried parents studied appears to exceed the national average by about 20 percent, in spite of the fact that many of them were less than 20 years old and were still attending school.[1] Thus, our clients at Vista Del Mar constituted at least one genre of unmarried parenthood that defies the stereotype of mental dullness as a characteristic of the unwed parent.

Social Class

Approximately 50 percent of the unmarried parents studied at Vista Del Mar were raised in upper-middle or lower-upper-class family environments. Another 45 percent were identified as lower-middle class. Only 5 percent were from lower-class families. Thus, the largest proportion of the study population came from the middle-class group, which predominates in our society. The public tends to believe that illegitimacy prevails almost exclusively among the lower classes of society, when, in fact, it is quite clear that the phenomenon is found throughout the class structure, including the presumably solid middle class.*

Religion

Vista Del Mar is a Jewish community service agency.

*This is not to deny, of course, that illegitimacy is more prevalent in various deprived and anomic populations.

Consequently, a large proportion of unmarried mothers who come to the agency to seek help, which often includes placing the baby for adoption with a Jewish family, are themselves Jewish. Not so for the unmarried fathers, however. When one remembers the fact that Jews generally marry Jews, the number of Jews who engage in illicit sexual relationships with non-Jews is surprising. In more than one-half of the couples included in our study, the mother was Jewish but the unmarried father was not (see Table 34).

In a study conducted in Los Angeles in 1959, religious intermarriage rates among Jewish families were reported as follows[2]: Husband Jewish, wife not Jewish–4.2%: wife Jewish, husband not Jewish–2.1%. A comparison of data on intermarriage in the Los Angeles study with interfaith unmarried partnerships in our study shows clearly that out-of-wedlock sexual relationships among our subjects differed drastically from prevailing Jewish marriage patterns. Some 65 percent of our couples were interfaith units, as compared with approximately 6 percent in the

TABLE 34. *Religion of Unmarried Mothers and Unmarried Fathers in the Study, by Partnership*

Religious Configuration	%
UM & UF both Jewish	24.8
UM & UF both non-Jewish	5.3
UM Jewish, UF non-Jewish	56.2
UM non-Jewish, UF Jewish	9.3
No data on religion of UF	4.4
Total	100.0
(No. of cases)	(226)

other study. This latter rate may have risen since 1959, but undoubtedly remains considerably below our 65 percent figure.

Also, at Vista Del Mar, the combination of female Jewish/male non-Jewish occurred more frequently than male Jewish/female non-Jewish. This is the opposite of intermarriage patterns generally found. Conclusions from such a finding must be viewed cautiously, however, since there are greater incentives for a Jewish unmarried mother to seek out a Jewish agency than for a non-Jewish mother to do so.

If choosing a partner of a different religion for sexual relationship is an indication of difficulty in the area of Jewish identity, then a larger proportion of unmarried Jewish mothers than fathers would appear to be in conflict with Mar study population of unmarried mothers may either respect to their Jewish heritage. Therefore, the Vista Del have been low in identification with Jewishness, or rebelling against Jewish values (see Table 35).[3]

TABLE 35. *Comparison of Vista Del Mar Unmarried Mothers 18 and Under with Those 19 and Over, on Jewish Identity Test*

Study Population	*Number*	*Mean Score**	*Standard Deviation*
Unmarried mothers 18 & under	49	77.3	2.81
Unmarried mothers 19 & over	54	84.2	2.70
(t=1.78; p=<.04, significant)			

*The higher the score, the further removed from Jewish identity.

Marital Status

Eighty percent of the mothers and 74 percent of the fathers in this study were unmarried. In regard to partnerships between unmarried couples, in 53 percent of them both partners were unmarried and neither partner had ever been married. Thus, in 47 percent of the partnerships, one or both were either married or had been married. In these latter relationships, therefore, one or both partners who entered into a relationship from which an illegitimate child resulted had had prior marital experience, and it may be inferred that they had some knowledge of sexual union and methods of preventing pregnancy. In these partnerships, therefore, lack of experience is not a reasonable explanation for the occurrence of out-of-wedlock pregnancy.

Previous Pregnancies

In 71 percent of the partnerships studied, the current out-of-wedlock pregnancy was the first for each partner. For the balance (29 percent), one or both parents had previously fathered or mothered one or more out-of-wedlock children. Recidivism is a factor, therefore, in out-of-wedlock pregnancy. Whether 29 percent is low or high depends upon one's point of view.

Parental Origins

Many studies of immigrants have pointed out that first-generation children are prone to deviate from the family's home country norms. Old-World ways are often rejected and new identities sought by first-generation children.

Although the percentage of unwed parents in the study

who were themselves foreign-born was minor, approximately one-fourth of their mothers and fathers *were* foreign-born. For some of the unmarried parents, this could have been a factor contributing to personal and social conflict. On the other hand, foreign lineage could be viewed as no more than a minor factor in accounting for the out-of-wedlock sexual behavior in our study subjects, since three-fourths of them were not children of foreign-born parents.

Personality Characteristics

Numerous tests have been developed by psychologists over the years to measure personality attributes. The pros and cons of personality measurements have frequently been noted, and testing itself has become a topic of public controversy. Of course, there is no one test that can be used universally. The selection of a test is a matter of judgment, based on the theoretical formulation of the test and the study objectives. In the study reported herein, the California Psychological Inventory[4] was employed because it is designed to "assess characteristics of personality which have a wide and pervasive applicability to human behavior and which, in addition, are related to the favorable and positive aspects of personality rather than to the morbid and pathological." In addition, the scales are "addressed principally to personality characteristics important for social living and social interaction."[5]

Thus, personality measures provided by the California Psychological Inventory deal with elements of personality that are generally relevant and that may, in addition, provide clues to preventive action. These measures of characteristics fall into four classes: 1) measures of poise, ascendancy, and self-assurance; 2) measures of socialization, maturity, and responsibility; 3) measures of achievement potential and intellectual efficiency; and 4) measures of intellectual and interest modes. Within each of these broad classes, there are specific scales of measurement. The findings presented here were obtained by administering the Inventory to unmarried parents, fathers as well as mothers.

The test profile chart (Figure 4) shows that personality profiles for unmarried fathers under twenty-one years of age and those for fathers over twenty-one followed the same general pattern. However, as might be expected, unmarried fathers over twenty-one scored higher (e.g., were more fully functioning) than those under twenty-one. For purposes of interpretation, the profile for unmarried fathers over twenty-one will be considered.

Personality Inventory Scores—Unwed Fathers

The unmarried father scored high in social poise, social presence, and self-acceptance, with peak scores ocurring for the two latter factors. His other scores were at or below the norm. What emerged was a profile of a person who is aggressive, persistent, verbally fluent, and inclined to be clever and enthusiastic. His highest score on the scale gives evidence of a tendency to be outspoken and self-centered. While his scores for these characteristics were not strikingly above the norm, they were sufficiently high to suggest that the unmarried father possess considerable social skill.

On the other hand, the unmarried father scored below the norm on scales measuring sense of well-being, social maturity, and responsibility. Although he had a high self-acceptance score, he also scored low on well-being, suggesting that he had a tendency toward defensiveness. Perhaps his current predicament contributed to feelings of self-doubt.

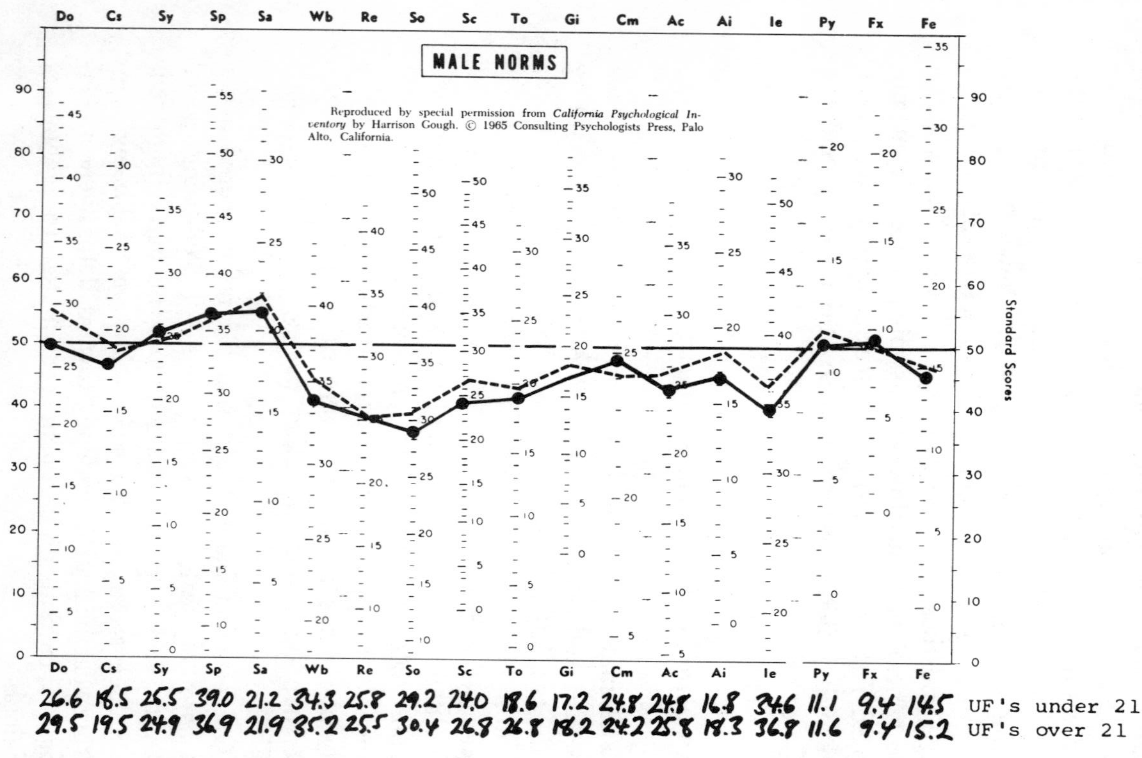

FIGURE 4. *Profile Sheet for the California Psychological Inventory: Male*

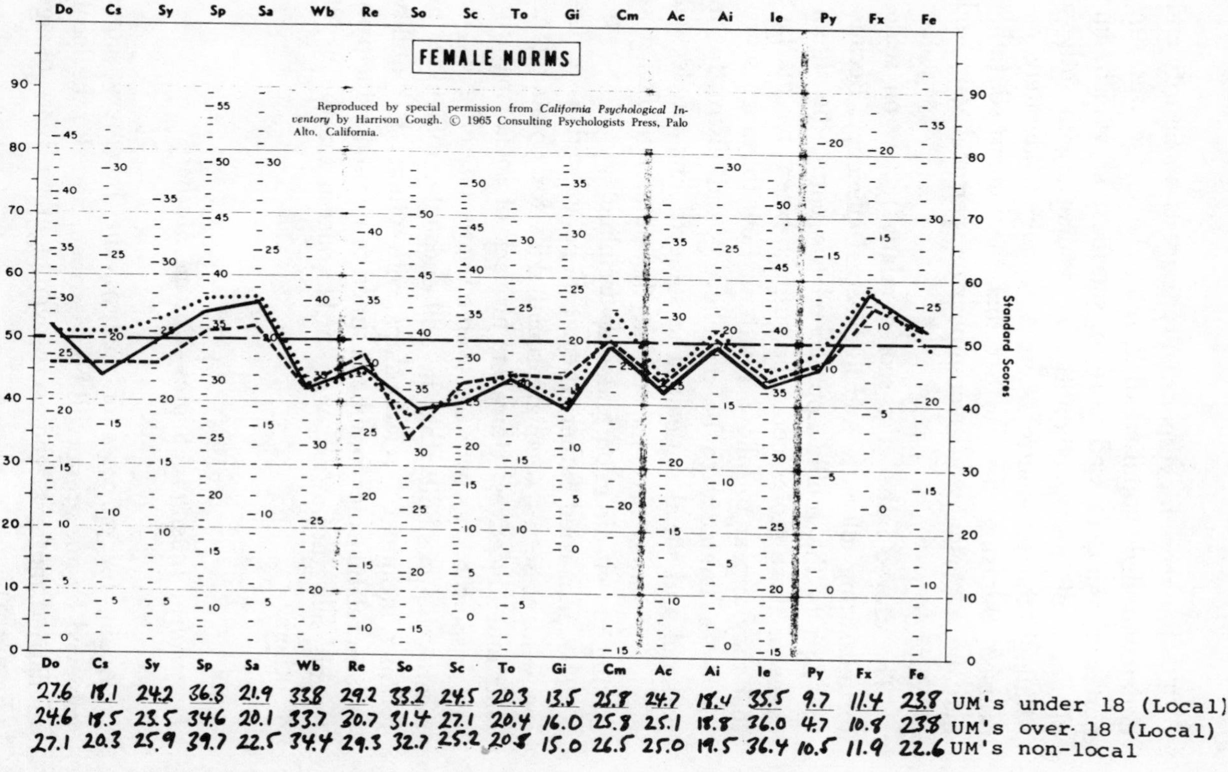

FIGURE 5. *Profile Sheet for the California Psychological Inventory: Female*

The low score for responsibility suggests immaturity and undercontrolled, impulsive behavior. The image was supported by the depressed score for socialization, with its implication of undependability in dealings with others. Although the self-control score was only moderately depressed, this suggested further that the unmarried father may be a person who overemphasizes personal gain and pleasure.

The unwed father also scored relatively low on scales for measuring tolerance and intellectual efficiency. Because the dips in the profile approached the norm, the significance of these scores could be suspect except for the fact that they appear to follow a pattern. Low tolerance scores suggest a tendency to be disbelieving and distrustful in personal and social outlook. The subjects' low intellectual efficiency scores may imply that the unmarried father is lacking in self-direction and self-discipline.

The unmarried father, then, can be viewed as a person who possesses adequate social skills for obtaining his ends and objectives. However, his lack of social maturity and responsibility, with an overemphasis on self-gain, indicates the possibility that he will encounter difficulties in forming meaningful relationships with others. His ability to form relationships may be destined to be used principally for his self-gratification, with little concern for the needs of others.

Personality Inventory Scores—Unwed Mothers

Again, for purposes of analysis, the Inventory scores achieved by one group will be described, namely, the local, unmarried mothers who were over eighteen years of age (Figure 5).

Scores that peaked above the norm were few. These peaks occurred on scales measuring social presence and self-acceptance, thus suggesting that the unmarried mother is moderately spontaneous, intelligent, aggresive, and self-centered. The most notable peak was on the flexibility scale, suggesting, among other implications, that the unmarried mother is concerned with personal pleasure and diversion.

Depressed scores occurred for well-being and socialization, indicating a tendency toward defensiveness and constriction in thought and action. Although the scores on scales measuring self-control, tolerance, good impression, achievement via conformity, and intellectual efficiency were only moderately depressed, a pattern of inadequacies persisted. There were hints in these scores that the unmarried mother has a tendency to overemphasize self-pleasure and personal gain; that she is too little concerned with the needs and wants of others; and that she tends to become disorganized under stress.

As we found with the unmarried father, the unmarried mother possesses moderate social skills, but her deficiencies in the area of responsibility and maturity suggest that she also may have problems in her relationships with others, particularly insofar as her ability to function may be oriented toward meeting her own needs without sufficient regard for the needs of others.

In neither profile were the peaks and valleys dramatic. Hence, the interpretations must be made with caution. However, the patterns in the two profiles were sufficiently similar to suggest that an unmarried father–unmarried mother constellation may exist. Both unwed parents appear to possess adequate social skills. Both scored low on the well-being, social maturity, and responsibility scales. It may be that illegitimate babies are more often born to partners who are deficient in the areas of maturity and responsibility and who lack deep concern for others.

Since very few studies have been conducted on unmarried fathers, comparative data from other inquiries are lacking. However, Clark Vincent, in his study of unmarried mothers, also employed the California Psychological Inventory and thus his findings provide comparative data for unmarried mothers.[6] The unwed mothers in the Vista Del Mar study scored significantly higher than those included in Vincent's study on the following scores. (A "t" score indicating significance at the .05 level was considered statistically significant.)

Measures of poise and self-ascendency:

	t
Dominance	3.72
Capacity for status	4.22
Sociability	4.23
Social presence	3.91
Self-acceptance	4.95

Measures of socialization and maturity:

	t
Responsibility	3.49
Tolerance	2.67
Communality	2.41

Measures of achievement potential:

	t
Achievement via conformity	2.63
Achievement via independence	4.68
Intellectual efficiency	3.42

Measures of intellectual and interest modes:

	t
Psychological mindedness	3.11
Flexibility	3.02

These results suggest that the unmarried mothers in the present study appeared to function more adequately as people than did Vincent's subjects. Particularly, the contrast is substantial in self-acceptance, achievement via independence, sociality, and capacity for status. As noted earlier, the subjects in our study came from predominantly middle-class families, and had demonstrated achievement in school and in other areas. They were, on the whole, an above-average group of subjects, whatever their current difficulties.

Those scales on which subjects in this study and those in Vincent's investigation did *not* differ significantly were:

	t
Sense of well-being	1.26
Socialization	0.21
Self-control	0.02
Good impression	0.55
Femininity	1.45

These five scales include several measures of importance in distinguishing unmarried parenthood, and lend indirect support to the thesis that, in spite of social class factors, certain aspects of personality—particularly self-control and socialization—are associated with the unwed parenthood status.

One other comparison substantiates the above conclusion. The Inventory scores of Vista Del Mar unmarried mothers who were of high-school age were compared with a cross section of female high-school students.[7] Here again, the group of unmarried mothers scored significantly higher on all scales of the California Psychological Inventory except for the scales of socialization, self-control, and good impression, on which their scores were significantly lower (for socialization $t=6.51$; for self-control $t=2.48$; and for good impression $t=2.29$).

Following the same clues as used above for comparing the unmarried mothers in our study with other high-school students and with another group of unmarried mothers, we compared the Inventory scores of this study's youthful unmarried fathers with the scores of a group of juvenile delinquents. The unmarried fathers scored higher on most scales except those measuring social maturity and responsibility.

Because begetting a child out of wedlock constitutes an act socially unacceptable in our culture, parents of illegitimate children are, in a sense, societal deviants, out of step with prevailing standards. It may be, therefore, that they share some characteristics with other deviants—those characterized as juvenile delinquents, for example, or those who have been placed in a correctional institution.

Our findings tend to bear out this hypothesis, since our unmarried parents' scores on the social maturity and responsibility scales of the California Psychological Inventory were similar to those achieved by juvenile delinquents and prison inmates.

Personal Disjunctions

To examine this theory further, we made use of a test developed by Richard Jessor. He suggested that certain characteristics or attributes of an individual may result in a predisposition to become a "deviant." One of these attributes he terms "disjunctions," which he describes as follows: "This concept refers to the disjunction ['gap'] between the life goals a person values and his expectations of being able to achieve these goals by the acceptable means provided by his culture."[8]

Jessor's measurement of disjuctions was derived from a list of 24 goals. The respondent was asked to indicate the importance of each goal and to indicate the extent to which he expected to reach this goal. In instances in which a goal was considered important and the subject's expectation of reaching it was negative, a personal disjunction was noted. Thus, a person who sees many of his wants in life as unattainable may come to harbor feelings of hopelessness and of low self-worth. On the other hand, an individual whose disjunction score is zero and who views all wants in life as attainable may be living in a fantasy-based world which could, in itself, represent an extreme reaction to hopelessness through denial.

We suggest that feelings of hopelessness, as measured by personal disjuction, may indicate that the individual is in the process of forming an identity or has established a strong negative identity. Furthermore, one who is low in self-esteem, and who sees needs and wants as being relatively unattainable, may also view as less important the need to assert self-control or responsibility and, in general, be deficient in social maturity and responsibility, the broad category in the California Psychological Inventory that was described earlier in this chapter, and in which the unmarried parents in our study consistently scored below the norm (see Table 36).

In Jessor's group of Anglo non-deviants, male and female, the norm fell at two to three personal disjunctions. It is evident from Table 36 that close to 50 percent of both

TABLE 36. *Frequency of Personal Disjunctions for Unmarried Parents in the Study, Expressed in Percentages*

Number of Disjunctions	*Unmarried Fathers %*	*Unmarried Mothers %*
0 - 1	33.3	26.3
2 - 3	21.1	21.1
4 - 20	45.6	52.6
Total	100.0	100.0
(No. of cases)	(57)	(118)

(X^2 0.73, df=1; $p > .70$, not significant)

our unmarried mothers and fathers indicated that they had four or more disjunctions. Furthermore, 33.3 percent and 26.3 percent of unmarried fathers and unmarried mothers, respectively, fell in the range of 0 to 1 personal disjunctions. Thus, only some 21 percent of the unmarried parents in our study fell within the norm for personal disjunctions established by the Anglo non-deviants tested by Jessor. The high proportion of unmarried parents who exhibited an abnormal number of personal disjunctions (either above or below the norm) suggests that these parents may harbor a sense of hopelessness in relation to attainment of their life goals, establishing thereby a psychological basis for deviant behavior.

Table 37 shows that the average (mean) number of disjunctions for the Vista Del Mar unmarried fathers was greater than the average for male non-deviants in Jessor's population, although the difference is not statistically impressive.

The same general findings appeared for Vista Del Mar unmarried mothers; i.e., they had a higher average number

TABLE 37. *Comparison of Mean Number of Disjunctions for Jessor's Group of Male Anglo-Saxon Non-Deviants and Vista Del Mar's Group of Unmarried Fathers*

Group	*Number of Subjects*	*Mean Score**
Jessor's	43	2.67
Vista Del Mar's	57	3.98
($t=1.21$, $p > .11$, near significance)		

*Standard deviations may be obtained by writing to the authors.

of personal disjunctions than did Jessor's group of female non-deviants but, again, the difference was statistically insignificant (Table 38).

In summary, results obtained by unmarried parents on the personal disjunction measurement tend to bear out the notion that these parents often have not sucessfully resolved conflicts centering about their life goals and expectations for the future.

TABLE 38. *Comparison of Mean Number of Disjunctions for Jessor's Group of Female Anglo-Saxon Non-Deviants and Vista Del Mar's Group of Unmarried Mothers*

Group	*Number of Subjects*	*Mean Score*
Jessor's	43	2.23
Vista Del Mar's	118	5.08
($t=1.63$; $p=.05$, not significant)		

Alienation

Jessor also noted that deviants show tendencies toward alienation, tend to lack social roots, and are inadequate in dealing with people, as measured by his alienation scale. We found little difference, in this, between our unmarried parents and Jessor's Anglo non-deviants, either male or female. This would tend to support the results we obtained by means of the California Psychological Inventory, indicating that unmarried parents display considerable social poise and a capacity for status—responses not generally linked with social alienation (Tables 39 and 40).

Attitude Toward Deviance

A further topic studied by Jessor was attitude toward deviance, i.e., the extent to which people explicitly accept or reject what society holds to be "right." Presumably a deviant would repudiate social norms as a way of reducing conflict within himself. Again, we compared scores obtained by unmarried parents in our study with those of Jessor's

TABLE 39. *Alienation Scores for Vista Del Mar Unmarried Mothers and Female Anglo-Saxon Non-Deviants*

Subjects	*Number of Subjects*	*Mean Score*
Vista Del Mar's unmarried mothers	119	15.38
Jessor's female Anglo-Saxon non-deviants	43	15.35

(t=.05, p=.48, not significant)

TABLE 40. *Alienation Scores for Vista Del Mar Unmarried Fathers and Male Anglo-Saxon Non-Deviants*

Subjects	*Number of Subjects*	*Mean Score*
Vista Del Mar's unmarried fathers	56	14.29
Jessor's male Anglo-Saxon non-deviants	25	15.19
(t=1.02, p=.15, not significant)		

group of non-deviant Anglo males and Anglo females using his attitude to deviance scale.[10] Although unmarried fathers were somewhat more inclined to view deviant actions as non-deviant than were Anglo-Saxon non-deviant males, the difference was not statistically significant (see Table 41). From Table 41, it is apparent that the unmarried fathers as a group tended to conform to social norms in their conceptions of what constitutes approved and disapproved behavior.

TABLE 41. *Attitude Toward Deviance—Jessor's Group of Anglo Male Non-Deviants and Vista Del Mar's Group of Unmarried Fathers*

Group	*Number of Subjects*	*Mean Score*
Jessor's Anglo male non-deviants	25	73.56
Vista Del Mar's unmarried fathers	57	68.90
(t=1.017, p=.15, not significant)		

Unmarried mothers, on the other hand, were less inclined to identify deviancy in accordance with norms and would, therefore, seem to deny in some measure the reality pressures of society (Table 42).

Home Environment

There is persistent evidence that identity problems, rooted in the home environment, affect unmarried parents. Several questionnaires were used to ascertain the views of the agency's social workers on home situations observed during interviews with unmarried parents. In addition, certain questions were asked of the unwed parents to obtain some clues concerning the home life of these individuals, with emphasis on relationships between parents and their children. In particular, they were asked to indicate the extent to which they saw their parents in conflict while in the home (Table 43).

TABLE 42. *Attitude Toward Deviance—Jessor's Group of Anglo Female Non-Deviants and Vista Del Mar's Group of Unmarried Mothers*

Group	*Number of Subjects*	*Mean Score*
Jessor's Anglo female non-deviants	43	88.88
Vista Del Mar's unmarried mothers	119	72.33

($t=6.4$, $p<.01$, significant)

TABLE 43. *Degree of Perceived Conflict Between Parents of Unmarried Parents*

Degree of Conflict Perceived	Assessors: Unmarried Mothers (%)		Assessors: Unmarried Fathers (%)	
Constant open conflict	8.6	34.4	13.3	42.2
Moderate open conflict	25.8		28.9	
Little open conflict	46.6	65.5	40.0	57.7
No open conflict	18.9		17.7	
Total	100.0*		100.0*	
(No. of cases)	(58)		(135)	

(X^2 computed by combining open conflict categories and little or no open conflict categories)
(X^2 1.65, df=1; $p > .20$, not significant)

*Rounded to 100.0%.

Around 42 percent of the unmarried mothers and 34 percent of the unmarried fathers indicated that their parents were in constant or moderate open conflict. These findings suggest that the unmarried parents studied either had a home life in which a great deal of conflict existed or that they perceived much conflict. Perhaps this conflict, perceived or real, is both symptom and cause of identity problems, particularly as they relate to clear identification with a positive male or female role. Erikson, in speaking about the process of ego identity and role attainment, notes:

> . . . Youths are now primarily concerned with what they appear to be in the eyes of others as compared to what they feel they are, and with the question of how to connect the role and skills cultivated earlier with the oc-

cupational prototype of the day. In their search for a new sense of continuity and saneness, adolescents have to refight many of the battles of earlier years, even though to do so they must artificially appoint perfectly well-meaning people to play the roles of enemies; and they are ever ready to install lasting idols and ideas as guardians of a final identity: here puberty rites 'confirm' the inner design of life.[11]

Since sexual identity develops during the maturation process, lack of sexual identity can flow from poor parental relationships and may be reflected in overt sexual behavior as an attempt at a solution. Caseworkers felt that for unmarried parents, such behavior represented a search for masculinity or femininity. This seemed to hold for unmarried fathers particularly (Table 44).

TABLE 44. *Frequency of Caseworkers' Assessment that Engaging in Sexual Relationships Proved Masculinity/Femininity to Unmarried Parents*

Proved Masculinity/ Femininity	*Unmarried Fathers** %	*Unmarried Mothers*** %
Yes	96.3	87.7
No	3.7	12.3
Total	100.0	100.0
(No. of cases)	(82)	(139)
(X^2 3.85, df=1; $p<.05$, significant)		

*Excludes 11 cases in which attitude was not assessed.
**Excludes 82 cases in which attitude was not assessed.

Psychosocial Profile of the Unmarried Father

Since little data exist on the unmarried father, developing a psychosocial profile of him was a key study objective. The frame of reference for doing so was Erik Erikson's concept, which deals with problems encountered in efforts to form an identity.[12] In our study, five indicators were developed to characterize persons with difficulties in identity formation:

1. Inability to function in a controlled society.
2. Inability to engage in a mature relationship with others.
3. Inner despair—lack of a sense of knowing where one one is going.
4. Inclination not to want recognition or approval from others.
5. Repudiation of societal norms.

Indicator 1: Inability to function in a controlled society. The unmarried fathers in our study usually had completed high school and were able to hold jobs effectively. The majority did not have a history of delinquent behavior. Profiles developed from Gough's California Psychological Inventory, however, suggested that they lacked certain ingredients necessary to full utilization of personal resources in an independent manner.[13]

The test results indicated that as a group they tended to be—to use sample California Psychological Inventory adjectives—"defensive," "rebellious," and "guileful" in dealing with others. The California Psychological Inventory scores also showed a tendency for them to be "immature," "disbelieving," "influenced by personal bias," and undercontrolled and impulsive in behavior. They were somewhat constricted in thought and action and inclined to overemphasize personal pleasure and self-gain.

Thus, the unmarried father emerges as one who may find difficulty in adjusting, not because he lacks intellectual ability or social skills, but because he is immature and irresponsible, factors possibly related to the absence of a strong, positive identity.

Indicator 2: Inability to engage in a mature relationship with others. Caseworkers reported that 95 percent of the unmarried fathers had fantasies concerning their abilities and self-image, showed over-romanticism toward their partners, and held impaired views of the relationship between cause and effect.

When caseworkers explored the meaning of the sex act, they ascertained that the unmarried father harbored feelings of guilt, of hostility toward his partner, and feelings that the unmarried mother was the aggressor. In only two cases (1.1 percent) was the unmarried father concerned with fear of pregnancy. Not using contraceptives and lack of concern about the possibility of pregnancy suggest immaturity in the sexual relationship.

For 85 percent of the cases, male caseworkers concluded that the sexual experience represented an effort by the unmarried father to prove his masculinity. This is further supported by our data, which indicate that 50 percent of the unmarried fathers in our study lived in homes where fathers were absent or deceased.

Indicator 3: Inner despair—lack of a sense of knowing where one is going. Eighty percent of the unmarried fathers either saw *all* their wants in life as attainable or *few* of their wants as attainable. Visualizing few wants as attainable suggests the existence of inner despair; visualizing all wants as attainable suggests a fantasy orientation toward life.

Indicator 4: Inclination not to want recognition or approval from others. Gough's Good Impression Scale identifies "persons capable of creating a favorable impression and who are concerned about how others react to them." We anticipated low scores in this scale for the unmarried fathers in our study. Results were not as predicted. Although the scores were below the norm for this attribute, they were not sufficiently depressed to suggest a clear disinclination on the part of the fathers to want approval of others. Furthermore, we found that 63 percent of the unmarried fathers believed the unmarried mother viewed their relationship as a love relationship. This suggests that the unmarried mother's approval and/or recognition were very important to the unmarried father.

Indicator 5: Repudiation of societal norms. When compared with a population of non-deviant males tested by Richard Jessor, the unmarried fathers in our study tended to view deviant and non-deviant acts according to societal norms. In addition, results of Jessor's Scale of Alienation showed that they did not regard themselves as alienated from society. Profile data were also gathered for the corresponding unmarried mother population. Essentially, the findings for the unmarried mothers were similar to those for the unmarried fathers. Unmarried mothers also scored low in the areas of responsibility and maturity, lacked strong feminine identity, and were low in self-esteem.

When neither sexual partner possesses a strong identity, and when neither is responsible and mature, each reinforces the other to satisfy personal needs with little regard for the consequences of the act.

Our study findings suggest that an unmarried father/mother constellation exists. Perhaps an individual becomes an unmarried parent when he or she is involved with a partner whose attributes fosters immature, sexually charged relationships.

Notes and References

1. *Readers' Digest Almanac.* Pleasantville, N.Y.: The Readers' Digest Association, Inc., 1966, p. 200.
2. *A Report on the Jewish Population of Los Angeles, 1959.* Los Angeles: Research Service Bureau, Jewish Federation Council of Greater Los Angeles, 1959.
3. Irving Sarnoff. "Identification with the Aggressor." *Journal of Personality,* 1951, p. 207.
4. Published by Consulting Psychological Press, Inc., Palo Alto, Calif.
5. Harrison G. Gough. *Manual for the Psychological Inventory.* Palo Alto, Calif.: Consulting Psychological Press, Inc., 1957, p. 7.
6. Clark E. Vincent. *Unmarried Mothers.* New York; The Free Press, 1961.
7. Gough, *op. cit.*, p. 35.
8. Richard Jessor. Unpublished paper, Institute of Behavioral Science, University of Colorado, Boulder, 1963.
9. Jessor, *op. cit.*
10. Jessor, *op. cit.*
11. Erik H. Erikson. *Childhood and Society.* New York: W. W. Norton and Co., Inc., 1950, p. 228.
12. Erik H. Erikson. *Psychological Issues I,* No. 1. New York: International Press, Inc., 1959.
13. Harrison G. Gough. California Psychological Inventory. Palo Alto, Calif.: Consulting Psychologists Press, Inc., 1956.

VIII The Parents

Because the problems of unmarried parents are interwoven with the attitudes, values, behavioral patterns, and child-rearing patterns of *their* parents, an understanding of these patterns may help toward a better understanding of the unmarried mother and father. Most teen-agers live at home and are financially dependent upon their parents. Since the pregnancy of a teen-aged girl living at home usually cannot be concealed from her parents, they become involved with all the ramifications of this event. The boy's parents soon become involved also, either through a legal or other confrontation with the girl's parents, or through the intervention of a social agency. Whatever may occur, we have found that parents of teen-agers, even more than teen-agers themselves, quickly recognize and respond to the tremendous implications of the fact that a child is to be born out of wedlock. Whereas the teen-aged girl, even when well along in pregnancy, may seem comfortable and not overly concerned about her predicament, her parents realize the serious implications of it and may be filled with tremendous anxiety.

The parents of an unwed father may seek legal recourse in an effort to protect their son. Often, they will deprecate the girl, attempting to place the blame upon her. Or, they may try to force the boy either to deny that he was involved with the girl or to say that other boys had also been sexually involved with her, thus implying that their son may not be the father of the child. These are the reactions of frightened, distraught parents, trying to protect their children. Too often, they fail to recognize that the children are growing up and moving toward educational pursuits, jobs and, eventually, independence, which may mean marriage and families of their own.

When confronted with an out-of-wedlock pregnancy, parents often react with genuine shock at the realization that their children are sexual beings who are about to become parents themselves. In acting out sexually, the children have acted as adults in an adult context, and now they find themselves confronted with adult problems. The parents often feel helpless and bewildered when they see their children faced with a complicated social problem which must, in some way, be resolved.

In many states, although a teen-aged unmarried mother may still be very much a child herself, she has the legal right to make the decision about what she will do with her baby. Thus, the girl, for the most part dependent upon her parents, is thrust into an area of complete independence. An element of control that the teen-ager has gained is brought into the open, since the law requires that she be told of her rights. This, in turn, may widen the gap between the teen-ager and her parents if the girl attempts to control, using the baby as a weapon. Parents need help in understanding and dealing with such a situation.

A social agency that helps families with these problems should not attempt to take over the role of the parents but try instead to help them carry out their own roles with their children, pointing out their obligation to examine the problem clearly and identifying various alternative solutions. It must recognize that, in many cases, the teen-aged mother will be returning to her home, and will continue to live with her parents, upon whom she is still dependent.

Such alternatives as marriage, adoptive placement, or rearing the child out of wedlock should be carefully explored with the couple's parents as well as with the unwed mother and father. Then, after some course of action has been decided upon, the agency should support the parents of the teen-agers and encourage them to make their position clear to their children. Too often this is not done, with the result that the unwed mother and father do not know where they stand and what they may realistically expect from their parents. Parents should be encouraged to state clearly what they will or will not be able to do in the situation. They should indicate how much money they will spend in providing medical care and living arrangements, how much support they will give should the teen-agers marry, and whether or not they would want to take the child into their home and rear him or help to rear him. A clear stand on the part of the parents can help the unwed parents to reach decisions about the baby and about their own future direction. Lack of a clear stand by parents can result in precipitous action by the teen-agers which could have little chance of success.

What Were the Parents of Our Unwed Parents Like?

Approximately 55 percent of the parents of the unwed parents in our study were alive and living together. For the unwed fathers, approximately 50 percent of their parents were not living together; either the parents were divorced, or one or both parents were deceased. Twenty-six percent of the fathers of our unmarried fathers had been married two or more times. In 45 percent of the cases, the parents of the unmarried parents were not living together or were deceased. This meant that the responsibility for rearing children in these cases had fallen to one parent (see Table 45).

TABLE 45. *Family Constellations of Parents of Unmarried Parents in the Study*

Family Status of Parents of Unmarried Parents	*Unmarried Fathers* %		*Unmarried Mothers* %	
Both parents alive and living together	51.4		58.8	
Parents divorced	25.0		23.5	
Father deceased	18.1	23.6	1.2	17.7
Mother deceased	1.4		5.3	
Both parents deceased	4.1		11.2	
Total	100.0		100.0	
(No. of cases)	(72)		(170)	

(X^2 computation by combining: father deceased, mother deceased, and both parents deceased)
(X^2 0.78, df=2; $p>.50$, not significant)

Approximately 72 percent of the unmarried mothers and fathers described their parents' marriages as happy (see Table 46). In Clark Vincent's study, 82 percent of the unmarried mothers who gave up their babies for adoption saw their parents as having a happy marriage.[1] (Although some of the unmarried mothers in our study kept their babies, the largest percentage placed them for adoption.)

A closer examination of parental relationships showed that for 41 percent of unmarried fathers, their fathers made most of the decisions in the family, while for 36 percent, the mothers made most of the decisions. In the balance of the cases, it appeared to the unmarried father that no one in his family took responsibility for making decisions. For 34 percent of the unmarried mothers, their fathers made the decisions in the family, whereas in approximately 32 per-

TABLE 46. *Unmarried Parents' Assessments of Their Parents' Marriages in Vista Del Mar Study*

Assessment of Happiness of Parental Marriage	*Assessors* Unmarried Fathers %	Unmarried Mothers %
Unusually happy	7.8	10.0
Very happy	20.3	22.9
Happy	35.9	32.9
Average in happiness (a bit above or below)	12.5	16.1
Unhappy	15.6	14.1
Very unhappy	7.9	4.0
Total	100.0*	100.0
(No. of cases)	(64)	(149)

(X^2 computation by splitting at happiness vs. unhappiness categories)
(X^2 0.11, df=1; $p > .70$, not significant)

*Rounded to 100.0%.

cent of the cases their mothers made the decisions. In the remaining cases, no particular parent took responsibility for making decisions (Table 47).

In approximately 58 percent of the cases, the unmarried father saw his father as the dominant parent, whereas 35 percent of the unmarried mothers saw their fathers as the dominant parent (see Table 48).

Approximately 34 percent of the unmarried fathers and 42 percent of the unmarried mothers stated that their parents were in constant or moderate open conflict (Table 49).

TABLE 47. *Focus of Decision-Making in Parental Unit*

Parent of Unmarried Parents Perceived as Making Most Decisions	*Unmarried Fathers* %	*Unmarried Mothers* %
Father	41.1	34.4
Mother	36.5	31.8
No particular parent	12.7	30.5
Someone else	9.5	2.6
Total	100.0*	100.0*
(No. of cases)	(63)	(153)

(X^2 15.05, df=3; $p > .01$, significant)

*Rounded to 100.0%.

TABLE 48. *Dominant Member of Parental Unit as Perceived by Unmarried Parents*

Parent Perceived as Dominant	*Unmarried Fathers %*	*Unmarried Mothers %*
Father	58.3	35.3
Mother	28.3	35.3
Other*	13.3	28.2
Total	100.0**	100.0**
(No. of cases)	(62)	(156)

(X^2 10.37, df=2; $p > .01$, significant)

*Example: sometimes one, sometimes the other.
**Rounded to 100.0%.

TABLE 49. *Degree of Perceived Conflict Between Parents of Unmarried Parents*

Degree of Conflict Perceived to Exist in Parental Household	*Unmarried Fathers* %		*Unmarried Mothers* %	
Constant open conflict	8.6	34.4	13.3	42.2
Moderate open conflict	25.8		28.9	
Little open conflict	46.6	65.5	40.0	57.7
No open conflict	18.9		17.7	
Total	100.0*		100.0*	
(No. of cases)	(58)		(135)	

(X^2 computed by combining open conflict categories and little or no open conflict categories)
(X^2 1.65, df=1; $p > .20$: not significant)

*Rounded to 100.0%.

Respondents in our study were asked to indicate how often they and their parents attended church or synagogue. The data would suggest that, in general, the unmarried parents in our study and their parents were only occasional church-goers or did not attend at all (Tables 50 and 51).

To what extent did the parents of the unmarried mothers and fathers see themselves as being in some way responsible for the out-of-wedlock pregnancy? We tried to ascertain this by asking them to what extent they were critical of themselves in their relationship with their son or daughter. Nearly 76 percent of the mothers and 68 percent of the fathers of the unmarried mothers were critical of themselves in relation to the rearing of their daughters. The majority of the parents of the unmarried fathers were

TABLE 50. *Frequency with Which Unmarried Mothers in the Study and Their Parents Attended Church/Synagogue*

Frequency of Attendance	*Unmarried Mother* %	*Unmarried Mother's Mother* %	*Unmarried Mother's Father* %
Weekly	5.9	5.7	5.5
2-3 times a month	2.3	5.7	3.0
Monthly	8.2	7.4	4.3
3-4 times a year	51.2	54.2	50.0
Never	32.2	26.8	37.2
Total	100.0*	100.0*	100.0*
(No. of cases)	(170)	(175)	(164)

(X^2 5.00, df=8; $p < .70$, not significant)

*Rounded to 100.0%.

TABLE 51. *Frequency with Which Unmarried Fathers in the Study and Their Parents Attended Church/Synagogue*

Frequency of Attendance	*Unmarried Fathers* %	*Unmarried Father's Mother* %	*Unmarried Father's Father* %
Weekly	10.1	23.6	13.4
2-3 times a month	13.0	2.8	1.5
Monthly	5.8	2.8	1.5
3-4 times a year	44.9	45.8	44.8
Never	26.1	25.0	38.8
Total	100.0*	100.0*	100.0*
(No. of cases)	(69)	(72)	(67)

(X^2 computation by combining weekly, 2-3 times a month, monthly, and 3-4 times a year)
(X^2 13.47, df=4; $p>.50$, not significant)

*Rounded to 100.0%.

critical of themselves and 68 percent were critical of themselves in relation to the rearing of their sons (Tables 52 and 53).

TABLE 52. *Extent to Which Parents of Unmarried Mothers (Under 18) Were Critical of Self Concerning Role in Relation to Daughter*

	Parents of Unmarried Mother	
	*Mother %**	*Father %***
Critical	68.6	55.9
Not critical	27.1	18.6
Does not apply****	4.3	25.4
Total	100.0	100.0***
(No. of cases)	(70)	(59)

(X^2 23.94, df=2; $p < .001$, significant)

*Excludes 7 cases in which worker was unable to assess factor.
**Excludes 8 cases in which worker was unable to assess factor.
***Rounded to 100.0%.
****Parent (s) of unmarried parents deceased or otherwise not living with family.

TABLE 53. *Extent to Which Parents of Unmarried Fathers (Under 21) Were Critical of Self Concerning Role in Relation to Son*

	Parents of Unmarried Father	
	*Mother %**	*Father %***
Critical	75.7	68.4
Not critical	8.1	7.9
Does not apply	16.2	23.7
Total	100.0	100.0

(X^2 not computable)

*Excludes 21 cases in which worker was unable to assess factor.
**Excludes 20 cases in which worker was unable to assess factor.

Closely associated with the parents' criticisms of themselves was the question of the extent to which they were concerned about what others might think of them as parents. Approximately 75 percent of the parents of the unwed fathers were quite concerned about this. In the case of the parents of the unmarried mothers, the figure was somewhat higher, approximately 82 percent (Tables 54 and 55).

Another way we attempted to ascertain the attitudes of the parents was to ask them whether or not they were concerned with what others might think of their pregnant daughter or son because of his predicament. Approximately 82 percent of the parents of pregnant girls were concerned about what others might think of the girl. This was also true for the parents of the boy, with approximately 70 percent of both parents being concerned about what others would think of their son's predicament (Tables 56 and 57).

TABLE 54. *Extent to Which Parents of Unmarried Mothers Were Concerned about What Others Would Think of Them as Parents*

	*Mother %**	*Father %***
Concerned	92.9	73.1
Not concerned	2.4	4.5
Does not apply	5.6	22.4
Total	100.0***	100.0
(No. of cases)	(71)	(67)

(X^2 not computable because expected cell frequencies less than 5 for 2 cells)

*Excludes 6 cases in which worker was unable to assess factor.
**Excludes 10 cases in which worker was unable to assess factor.
***Rounded to 100.0%.

Table 55. *Extent to Which Parents of Unmarried Fathers Were Concerned about What Others Would Think of Them as Parents*

	*Mother %**	*Father %***
Concerned	77.5	70.7
Not concerned	7.5	9.8
Does not apply	15.0	19.5
Total	100.0	100.0
(No. of cases)	(40)	(41)

(X^2 not computable)

*Excludes 18 cases in which worker was unable to assess factor.
**Excludes 17 cases in which worker was unable to assess factor.

Table 56. *Extent to Which Parents of Unmarried Mothers Were Concerned about What Others Would Think of Their Pregnant Daughter*

	*Mother %**	*Father %***
Concerned	92.9	72.7
Not concerned	2.8	4.5
Does not apply	4.2	22.7
Total	100.0	100.0
(No. of cases)	(71)	(66)

(X^2 not computable)

*Excludes 6 cases in which worker was unable to assess factor.
**Excludes 6 cases in which worker was unable to assess factor.

TABLE 57. *Extent to Which Parents of Unmarried Fathers Were Concerned about What Others Would Think of Their Son*

	*Mother %**	*Father %***
Concerned	77.5	64.3
Not concerned	7.5	14.3
Does not apply	15.0	21.4
Total	100.0	100.0
(No. of cases)	(40)	(42)
(X^2 not computable)		

*Excludes 18 cases in which worker was unable to assess factor.
**Excludes 16 cases in which worker was unable to assess factor.

The parents, then, of the unmarried mother and unmarried father were able to grasp the seriousness of the situation perhaps more than their sons or daughters, and they expressed a great deal of concern about it and about what others would think of it.

Notes and References

1. Clark E. Vincent. *Unmarried Mothers.* New York: The Free Press, 1961, p. 189.

IX The Role of the Social Worker

Direct services to unmarried mothers and, more recently, to unmarried fathers, have been developed under the auspices of social agencies, both private and public. These services are primarily provided by social caseworkers employed by the agencies. Other disciplines, such as psychiatry, psychology, education, public health, and nursing, often become involved in the team effort to help unmarried parents. The primary person, however, remains the social caseworker, whose job is not only to counsel the unmarried parent and his family directly, but to be aware of community resources and to utilize them in behalf of his client. In this chapter we shall examine in detail the social worker's role in working with unwed parents.

The following premises are basic to formulating approaches to working with the unwed father and mother[1]:

1. The growing child's fundamental needs for nurturing and for sex and role identification are best met in the family structure as we know it today—man and woman marrying, establishing a home together, and rearing children, each assuming fairly well defined roles and responsibilities.
2. With the conception of an out-of-wedlock child, a man and woman have created the roles of mother, father, and child outside of the socially useful structure of the protective family unit. The usual provisions have not

been made for nurturing or for sex and role identification. The reality of the child immediately raises the question of where and how these needs shall be met.

3. Unwed parents usually realize, or can be helped to realize, that they have participated in creating a serious problem and, underlying what may be surface defenses, they usually wish to have help in meeting their responsibilities and in gaining a better understanding of the problem. Essentially, responsibility must be met by providing for the child's needs, as well as by showing concern and consideration for the other partner. The child's needs may be met either by adoptive placement or by retaining continued rights and responsibilities for rearing the child.
4. Making decisions about the future of the child becomes the key problem that must be faced. The social worker understands that the infant has an unconscious meaning for both parents and that it may represent a neurotic solution to emotional problems. It is often from the unwed parents' reaction to the pregnancy and the infant that we gain insight into their life problems. With this knowledge, we may more realistically help to examine how the child may have represented a solution and in what direction real—not fantasized—help for themselves and the child may lie.
5. In working with the unmarried mother and father, the social worker is the one who consistently represents reality, offering help where it may be given, e.g., hospital care, exploration of community resources, help with legal, educational and vocational decisions, and sex education. Therapeutic attention to the problem is greatly facilitated by the drama of the situation, with its progression from conception to gestation and birth.
6. In times of crisis, a person or group becomes more susceptible to the influence of the helping process. During

the pregnancy crisis, help, rationally directed and purposefully focused, may be more effective than extensive help given at a period when the principals are less emotionally involved. Although other chronic problems of an intrapsychic nature may also exist and may require long-term counseling, the acute problem—the pregnancy—cannot be put aside. Therefore, the caseworker must offer immediate, concrete service to the client at the point of crisis. Time spent with the unmarried parent must be both purposeful and efficiently utilized. This may mean that the caseworker is more directive and assertive than he might otherwise be.

7. An affirmative position that states some positive moral, ethical, and psychological values that provide direction for mature and satisfying family life is fundamental to a constructive approach in working with problems created by illegitimate pregnancy. In a society that too often emphasizes the excitement and thrill of illicit love, sex needs to be depicted as part of a total love relationship, with its corollaries of responsibility to one another, marriage, and child rearing. The licit sexual relationship must be upheld and strengthened, as having the greatest potential for fulfilling the individual's need for intimacy, acceptance, and sexual satisfaction with trust and without inhibitions.

In addition to understanding these premises, the social worker needs to understand specific areas in which the unmarried father can help. Frequently, the unwed father asks, "I am concerned about her pregnancy and the fact that a child is going to be born, but what can I do about it? After all, she is going to have the child." When responding to questions like this, the social worker should indicate specific ways in which the unmarried father can help, including:

1. Standing by the unmarried mother. This lends some dignity to the relationship and is of extreme importance to the mother.
2. Participating in planning for the child's care and future.
3. Assuming and meeting financial responsibility.
4. Examining the life problems revealed by the illegitimate pregnancy.
5. Recognizing the meaning and responsibilities of marriage and parenthood.
6. Understanding his attitude toward the child's mother.
7. Understanding his attitude toward sex and the meaning of sexual relations.
8. Recognizing his attitude toward fatherhood.

In the implementation of the premises that are basic to formulating the agency's approaches to its work with the unmarried father, social work activity follows a well-defined process that essentially falls into the following categories: 1) reaching out to the unmarried father; 2) involving the unmarried father in a meaningful relationship with the agency; 3) ascertaining what the unmarried father will need to do in this situation, and what the caseworker will need to do through intervention, i.e., selection of casework goals, and implementation of goals by the unmarried father and the worker; 4) assessment with the unmarried father about what occurred during the casework relationship and its meaning for the future; and 5) a discussion of sex education.

Reaching Out to the Unmarried Father

To reach out to the unmarried father effectively, the worker must be committed to an aggressive approach in which he actively seeks out the father and encourages him, in an assertive manner, to accept agency services. This is an essential ingredient of the social work process; without it, the direct involvement of the unmarried father becomes unlikely. Thus, the worker must move away from the traditional social work approach in which the responsibility for seeking help has been placed upon the potential client. He must reach out to the client by explaining the ways in which the agency can help and by presenting concrete reasons why the client should accept these services. This kind of approach is not new. Mary Richmond established it as a method in the early days of social work. Currently, other agencies, notably O.E.O. programs, are utilizing it to aggressively sell their programs, and their workers knock on doors seeking clients.

Concomitant with the process of reaching out, the worker must indicate to the father what agency services are available to him, and explain the implications of accepting or not accepting these services. Thus, the social worker must be willing to reach out to the father and intervene aggressively in the casework process, clarify the agency practices and policies, and set forth the conditions under which the client can expect to be treated as a parent in solving his problems. (Specific methods that may be used in reaching out to unmarried fathers are delineated in Chapter IV).

Involving the Unmarried Father in a Meaningful Relationship with the Agency

Reaching the unmarried father and bringing him into the agency for services is only the beginning. If he is to be helped, he must become an active participant in the social work process. As was pointed out in Chapter IV, this involvement is partially accomplished when he is highly motivated by the unmarried mother to seek agency help.

By involvement we mean that the unmarried father needs to recognize that a problem exists—a problem that he had a vital part in creating. He needs to accept this responsibility and become motivated to examine his inner needs and to take steps to ameliorate the situation. Recognition by the unmarried father that a problem exists in which his involvement is an important part of the solution, can come about most effectively through the social worker's intervention.

Sometimes the father's involvement may be gained through discussion. In other instances, it may be necessary for the worker to confront him with stark reality—not as a threat, but as a way of honestly looking at problems that can occur if responsible action is not taken. Some of the reasons for the unmarried fathers' continued involvement with the agency, as measured by continuity of agency contacts, are documented in Table 58.

Given the fact that involvement is an important aspect of the casework process, some selected information on the effects of involving unmarried fathers in the study may be in order.

The involvement of the unmarried fathers has positive effects on the unmarried mother, particularly on her adjustment to the pregnancy. In our study, these effects included helping the unmarried mother to gain a better understanding of: 1) the factors leading to parenthood; 2) her relationship to the father; 3) the external factors contributing to her experience. Frequently, the mother also gained a better understanding of the implications involved in bearing a child, and behaved more responsibly in dealing with her problem. These findings reflect caseworkers' assessments of

TABLE 58. *Extent to Which Various Motivational Factors Contributed Toward Unmarried Fathers Keeping Agency Appointments, by Age Category (Caseworkers' Assessments)*[*]

Reason for Keeping Appointment	*Age of Unmarried Father* Under 21 % (N)	Over 21 % (N)
Continued pressure by worker	43.1 (25)	27.8 (10)
Parental pressure	21.0 (12)	5.6 (2)
Outside pressure (law enforcement, etc.)	17.5 (10)	2.8 (1)
Pressure of unmarried mother	24.1 (14)	16.7 (4)
Pressure of unmarried mother's parents	3.4 (2)	0.0 (0)
To reduce possibility of legal sanctions	24.1 (14)	16.7 (6)
To meet agency expectations	69.0 (40)	55.6 (20)
Because results helpful to unmarried mother	63.8 (38)	66.7 (24)
Because results helpful to him (i.e., unmarried father)	74.2 (43)	69.4 (23)

[*]Percentage computations include "does not apply" responses; computations do not include "no answer" responses.

the effects on the unmarried mother when the unmarried father also receives casework services by the agency.

Similarly, in our study the unmarried father also made personal gains from his involvement with the agency. He was helped to: 1) understand the problems involved in bringing a new human being into the world; 2) behave responsibly in dealing with the problems of unwed parenthood; and 3) develop a realistic relationship (or a termination of relationship) with the unmarried mother.

Many of the unwed fathers seen during the project were also helped to discuss their sexual knowledge with their social workers. These discussions covered various topics including contraceptive devices, when this topic was appropriate, and were followed up with a referral to the Planned Parenthood Association. Similar discussions also took place with the unwed mothers. Without moralizing, condemning, or deprecating the sexual experience, the social workers were able to discuss sex and to answer questions about it directly and frankly. Many of the unmarried fathers viewed sex, at its best, in technical and mechanical terms: they saw it as something that one does (often because others are doing it), rather than as something that one experiences and has deep feelings about. In these discussions, the importance of the relationship aspect of sex, of consideration of the partners for each other, of commitments to the future, and of readiness to assume responsibilities for one's actions were carefully discussed.

A large majority of the unwed fathers in our study knew about contraceptives, but they had seldom used them when having sexual relations. Typical responses, when asked why a contraceptive was not used, were: "Yes, I know all about this, but to have used a contraceptive would have been just having sex for its own sake, and our relationship was different." "She wasn't that kind of girl." "When one gets married, he uses contraceptives. When I get married I'll use them too."

When contraceptives had been used, the fact that they had to be used "religiously" had eluded most of the unwed fathers and, when this was made explicit, a very forthright discussion about contraceptives usually followed. The connection between sexual relations and having babies had also eluded many of the unwed fathers, particularly the teenagers. The fact that sexual relations can be an enjoyable, positive experience in one's life without producing unwanted offspring needed to be discussed more fully with the fathers, as did their responsibility in preventing pregnancy. Many were surprised to learn that achieving a satisfactory sexual adjustment in marriage often takes many months, sometimes years, to achieve.

Finally, the fact that sexual intercourse is a very intimate experience between two people, and that the pleasure can be enhanced as the marriage matures was also discussed. A good number of unwed fathers who viewed the sexual experience in simplistic and often negative terms were helped to understand that it can be a positive experience that can grow in meaning and richness.

Ascertaining Clients' Needs and the Selection of Appropriate Goals

Implicitly or explicitly, caseworkers set goals for themselves and for their clients. These goals may be entered into jointly by caseworker and client, or by the caseworker alone. For the casework experience to be meaningful to the client, however, goals should be shared with him and some at least should be seen as attainable. Frequently, the attainment of a goal with a concrete referent can serve as a stepping stone to attaining a conceptual type of goal.

Goals selected should relate to the client's needs. When an unmarried father is the client, these goals may be related also to the needs of the unmarried mother of his child. The goals that were established as guidelines for the social workers serving the unmarried fathers and mothers in this demonstration study were:

1. To involve the unmarried father's parents in a relationship with agency (e.g., to bring parent(s) to Vista Del Mar).
2. To help the unmarried father understand the factors in himself that led to illegitimate parenthood.
3. To help the unmarried father understand factors *in others* that led to the out-of-wedlock pregnancy (e.g., personality of unmarried mother, social factors, etc.).
4. To help the unmarried father understand the implications involved in bringing a new human being into the world.
5. To help unmarried fathers to behave responsibly in dealing with problems of parenthood.
6. To help the unmarried father develop a realistic relationship (or termination of the relationship) with the unmarried mother.
7. To help the unmarried father to develop personality qualities that will prevent him from repeating his mistake.
8. To help the unmarried father maintain agency contact until the birth of the baby.
9. To help the unmarried father to be supportive and helpful to the unmarried mother during her pregnancy.
10. To motivate the unmarried father to participate in making the appropriate decision about the baby's future.
11. To help the unmarried father to make the appropriate decision with respect to his own future.
12. To motivate the unmarried father to assume his share of the responsibility by making financial contributions for medical and maternity costs.
13. To help the unmarried father to understand his own

rights, and those of the unmarried mother, concerning decision-making with respect to the baby.

Parenthetically, these goals, which were developed following extensive interviews with social workers, proved to be exhaustive. But the articulation of goals for agency practice can provide a helpful tool in sharpening casework skills and in providing uniformity of service for agency clientele.

Implementation of Goals

The caseworkers in our study exerted much effort to achieve the stated goals for our work with unmarried fathers. Because of the many variables involved, implementation of the goals differed depending upon the particular father.

Certainly, complex goals requiring many interviews over a long period of time were inappropriate for a situation in which the unmarried father visited the agency a limited number of times. Then, too, the personal characteristics and degree of motivation of each unmarried father had to be considered. Sometimes a selected goal had to be discarded when a precipitous severing of agency relationship occurred, or when the goal selected proved to be one which had little meaning or interest to the unmarried father.

We found, through experience, that the goals most effectively implemented were those in which:

1. Goal referents were simple and did not require the client to deal with high-level conceptual thinking.
2. Goal referents were reality based and easily identifiable with existing societal norms.
3. The application of "crisis theory" whereby pregnancy out of wedlock is seen as an event where, "a little help, rationally directed and purposefully focused at a strategic

time, is more effective than more extensive help given at a time of lesser emotional accessibility."[2]

In conclusion, workers must take the time to examine agency goals and methods of implementing them if their service to unwed parents is to be effective and dynamic.

Notes and References

1. Matile Rowan and Reuben Pannor. "An Assertive Casework Approach to the Older Unmarried Father." *Child Welfare.* Child Welfare League of America, Inc., March, 1961.
2. Lydia Rapoport. "Working With Families in Crisis: An Exploration in Preventive Intervention." *Social Work*, 7, No. 3, July, 1962, p. 49.

X Prevention

The study of the prevention of out-of-wedlock pregnancy should be undertaken concomitantly with the study of the problems of unmarried parenthood.

Many authorities advance the opinion that prevention of unwed parenthood can be substantially reduced through wider education about contraceptives and the dissemination of contraceptive devices.[1] This view is superficial in that it ignores the fact that underlying dynamics are important contributing factors to out-of-wedlock pregnancy.[2] The following quotation supports this statement:

> Despite increasing sophistication, complexities and problems in the use of contraceptives persist. One arresting paradox is the number of unintended pregnancies that occur despite the availability of contraceptives. Some young adults are simply ignorant of the relevant facts. Others, familiar with the information, fail to act in accordance with it for reasons based in unconscious motivation and conflict.[3]

In this study, we approached the subject of prevention through an evaluation of the answers given by our unwed parents on the California Psychological Inventory. In addition, we asked caseworkers to identify factors revealed by the Inventory and by relevant statements of the unwed parents that they thought might have prevented the out-of-wedlock pregnancy.

Factors Caseworkers Thought Might Have Prevented Out-of-Wedlock Pregnancies

For both unmarried fathers and unmarried mothers, caseworkers identified factors indicative of impaired family relationships, either between parents or between parents and child (see Figure 6). These included impaired com-

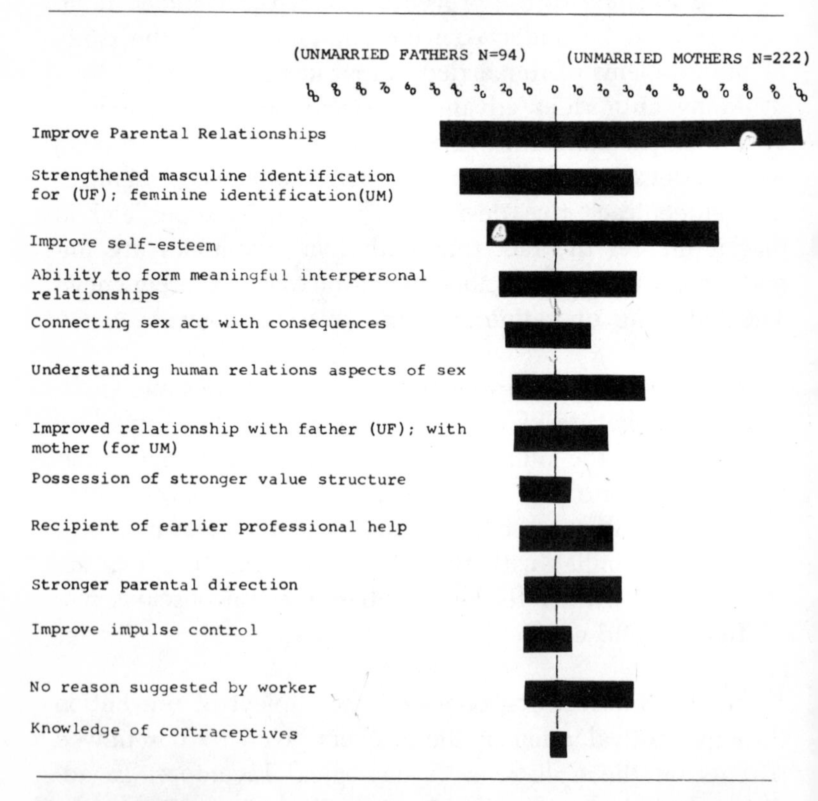

FIGURE 6. *Preventive Factors that Might Have Mitigated Against Out-of-Wedlock Pregnancy for Unmarried Fathers and Unmarried Mothers, as Seen by Caseworkers*

munication with parents, lack of parental interest in their children, need for value structure in the family, over-emphasis on permissiveness, and inconsistencies on the part of parents in their methods of handling discipline.

Lack of masculine or feminine identity was cited by case-workers for both of the unwed parents, but this factor was cited more frequently for unmarried fathers than for un-married mothers. Since sexual identity develops during the maturation process, lack of sexual identity can flow from poor parental relationships.

The assessment of the need for masculine identity as a deterrent against fathering an out-of-wedlock child was ex-pressed by Futterman and Livermore in 1947.[4] Of potential significance was the frequency with which lack of masculine identity was chosen by male caseworkers as contributing toward out-of-wedlock pregnancy. It is conjectured from this finding that the unmarried father may be motivated, con-sciously or unconsciously, to create a child as proof of his masculinity. The same conclusion was arrived at in the previously cited recent study of college students:

> The boy who carries out sexual intercourse without con-traception also is likely to be expressing one or more un-conscious attitudes. He may be unsure of his masculinity and feel unconsciously that fathering a child will prove his virility.[5]

Similarly, the unmarried mother may be motivated to pro-duce a child as proof of her femininity.

Lack of self-esteem was also given high priority as a factor contributing to illegitimacy for both unmarried fathers and unmarried mothers. Low self-esteem is inextricably related to weak masculine or feminine identity. In our culture, an individual cannot normally gain self-esteem without a strong masculine or feminine identity.

Impaired masculine/feminine identity on the part of unwed parents, along with low self-esteem, may be a reflection of problems currently prevalent in our society. Pollack suggests that a redefinition of male/female roles may be required:

> From this vantage point I would like to suggest that the setting of therapeutic goals may have to shift from its current emphasis on strengthening the male and weakening the female . . . to a relationship between sexes in which deference can be acknowledged without the need to associate it with a relationship of superordination and subordination.[6]

Another factor that received high priority was the need for both unmarried fathers and unmarried mothers to form more meaningful interpersonal relationships. This factor is closely allied with impaired parental relationships, low self-esteem, and weak masculine/feminine identity.

Knowledge of contraceptives was identified as the least important deterrent to out-of-wedlock pregnancy for both unmarried fathers and unmarried mothers.

Things Unwed Fathers and Mothers Would Have Done Had They Been Their Parents

Unmarried Fathers

The greater proportion of identified answers to these questions fell into the category of "would have established a better relationship with family." For example:

1. Would have established better relationship with son.
2. Would have engaged in less arguing.
3. Would have been more attentive to the needs of the children.
4. Would have tried to keep the family together.
5. Would have been a more dominant father.

These responses reinforce the observations made by the caseworkers, as shown in Figure 6 which lists "improve parental relationships" as the most important factor in prevention of out-of-wedlock pregnancies.

The second most frequent category of responses was "would be more considerate of spouse." This could suggest two things: 1) failure of the unwed fathers' fathers to provide a masculine image; or 2) over-identification of the unwed fathers with their mothers. Again referring to Figure 6, it can be seen that workers cited "stronger masculine identification" as being the second most important factor in preventing illegitimacy.

The third most frequent responses were in the category of "would be less permissive with children." In some respects, this relates to "better relationships with family," but it also suggests the failure of the father to spell out and follow through on expectations. Identity development could well be hampered under such conditions. This was also considered an important change the unwed father would have wished in his mother. Failure of the mother to be definitive in setting expectations could well be a form of indulgence causing additional problems in role identifications.

Unmarried Mothers

For unmarried mothers, the majority of responses fell into the category of "better relationships with family." Impressions of the workers concerning importance of better family relationships as a preventive factor continued to be confirmed as important by the unmarried parents as they assessed their impressions of family life.

Unmarried mothers indicated next frequently that they would have been less permissive. This pattern duplicates that reported above for the unmarried father.

Had the unmarried mother been her father, she would have been a more responsible person. Had she been her mother, she would have been concerned with being more considerate of spouse and would have been in the home more often.

Preventive Recidivism Among Unmarried Fathers

Bringing the unmarried father into the picture may be seen as a way of reducing recidivism. When the unmarried father becomes a partner with the unmarried mother in attempting to solve their problem, both are exposed to the following experiences:

1. Exploration of the meaning of the sexual experience.
2. Confrontation of the realities involved in bringing an out-of-wedlock child into the world. This may include seeing the baby, thus reinforcing the movement from fantasy to inescapable reality.
3. Exploration of the unmarried father's and mother's readiness for taking on the responsibilities of marriage and parenthood.
4. Assumption by the unmarried father of responsibility for helping to meet medical and hospital costs resulting from the pregnancy.

Some Approaches to Prevention of Illegitimacy

Approaches to the prevention of illegitimacy could include extensive psychological testing of school children as a basis for developing programs of group counseling. Such counseling would be geared particularly to those children who show low performance in social maturity and responsibility. These programs, in addition to helping to reduce the potential for illegitimacy, would have value in connection with a variety of other personal and social issues. Also to be considered is the selection by agencies of casework goals and methods that will help unmarried parents to strengthen their personality integration, particularly in areas of responsibility and self-control.

Because both unmarried mothers and fathers scored low on social maturity and responsibility, preventive methods must take into account the role that psychological factors play in illegitimacy. Knowledge of contraceptive devices may be viewed as useful in preventing out-of-wedlock pregnancy when—and only when—the individual possesses attitudes that make the use of such devices feasible. Encouraging unwed parents to assume greater responsibility for their actions calls for emphasis on:

1. The development of clearer laws that define the responsibilities of unwed parents to each other and to their out-of-wedlock child.
2. The extension of services to unmarried fathers in which the implications of having a child out of wedlock are stressed, together with firm expectations that the fathers will assume responsibility for their actions. Such services

may act as a deterrent to recidivism and have a positive impact upon the peers of the unmarried fathers.

3. A more cautious approach by authorities to the subject of contraceptives as a deterrent to pregnancy. Use of contraceptives is undoubtedly effective in preventing pregnancies when the users possess maturity and the psychological authority required for successful usage. Contraception requires time, privacy, assurance, and conscious recognition of the sexual act and its consequences. It also requires ability to deal with reality, to plan ahead, and to have a conscious recognition of the needs and wants of others.
4. A promulgation through various media and communication channels of the concept that behavior which may lead to an out-of-wedlock pregnancy deserves as much attention from parental and other authorities as an out-of-wedlock pregnancy itself. Frequently, the fact that teen agers are engaged in premarital sexual relations is known and accepted with little censure, but when a pregnancy occurs, punitive actions are often taken.
5. An expansion of family life and sex education programs by educational and welfare organizations with emphasis given to: concern with the wants and needs of others; concern with the emotional aspects of sexual relations; and teaching sex as an emotionally laden experience rather than a mechanical act disassociated from meaningful interpersonal relationships.

Prevention of unwed parenthood is a complex undertaking. It must be concerned with problems that result from ill-defined family relationships, with the confusion and contradiction between stated values and what is practiced, and with the struggle by youth for an identity.

Notes and References

1. Sidney Furie. "Birth Control and the Lower-Class Unmarried Mother." *Social Work II*, No. 1, January, 1966, pp. 42-49.
2. Reuben Pannor and Byron W. Evans. "Family Planning and Illegitimacy." *Social Work*, Letters to the Editor, July, 1966, p. 125.
3. *Sex and the College Student*. The Committee on the College Student, Group for the Advancement of Psychiatry. New York: Atheneum Publishers, 1966, p. 52.
4. Samuel Futterman, M. D. and Jean B. Livermore. "Putative Fathers." *Journal of Social Casework XXXIII*, May, 1947, p. 175.
5. *Sex and the College Student. Op. cit.*, p. 55.
6. Otto Pollack. "Family Structure: Implications for Mental Health." *The Social Worker*, Canada, October- November, 1964, p. 78.

Black Star, Werner Wolff

The Unmarried Father: From Shadow to Reality: Part III

A tall, handsome, neatly dressed young man sat quietly in the reception room of the adoption agency waiting to see the social worker. He felt nervous and anxious, just as he had five years before when he had sat in the same room waiting to see the same social worker.

At that time, he had been a gangly, 17-year-old adolescent. He had gotten a 15-year-old girl pregnant. The baby, a girl, had been placed for adoption.

It seemed that each year following the adoption, he had found himself thinking more and more about the baby. In fact, he had never stopped thinking about her. He learned through a friend that the baby's mother, Betty, was now happily married, and the mother of a child. He knew what she had gone through with her first baby, and how difficult it had been for her to place it for adoption. He was glad she was happily married, and that she now had a child of her own. He was sure that in some way this helped her get over the fact that her first baby had been placed for adoption.

He had not been that lucky. After graduating from high school, he had gone on to college, where he had decided to become a teacher. Teaching children was a demanding but satisfying job. Yet it was not so absorbing that he did not think about his daughter a great deal. He wondered what she looked like when she took her first step, what her first words were, what she looked like in her first dress.

He wished that it was he and not someone else whom she could call "Daddy." She must be in kindergarten now. He was sure she was beautiful. He would give anything to be able to hold her, to take her by the hand for a walk. He hoped he might be able to see her, perhaps just catch a glimpse of her but, if that was not possible, maybe he could do something for her that would make her life easier. He was working now, he had money, and he wanted to do something for his child.

The social worker remembered Don and greeted him in a warm, friendly manner. He seemed genuinely glad to see him. He asked Don about his work, his parents, his social life. He wondered why he wasn't dating more, and what his thoughts were about getting married.

Don replied that it wasn't easy to find the right person, and he didn't really feel ready for marriage. He was more anxious to talk about the child, who was now five years old. Lately, he had found himself constantly thinking about her. This was what had finally brought him back to the agency.

The infant girl that Don and Betty had relinquished for adoption five years before had been placed with a couple who were in their late twenties. They had been married for five years, but had been unable to have a child of their own. Ironically, Don and Betty's misfortune as teen-agers had given this couple joy and happiness. They loved the little girl very much. Before she had started school, they had told her that she was adopted. They had explained to her that she had grown inside another mother, but that mother, who was not able to take care of her, had asked the adoption agency to find a mother and father who could.

The adoptive parents knew that as she grew older, she would ask more questions about her mother and father—about why they had not been able to get married, why they had given her up for adoption, what kind of people they were, and what they looked like. The social worker assured Don that the family who had adopted his little girl would be able to answer these questions; that they were very comfortable with their adopted child; and that they would be able to explain to her, as they had already begun to do, what being adopted meant, and what her natural parents were like.

What did Don think they should tell her about her real father? Don thought for a while and finally said, "I hope they can tell her good things about me. I know I've made mistakes, but if I hadn't made that mistake with Betty, that couple never have our little girl. Yet I would like her to think of Betty and me as good people who loved her very much, and who only wanted the best for her. We wanted her to have a family, a home, security, stability, all the things neither of us could have given her. We weren't ready for marriage, and if we had been forced into it it would have been wrong and probably would have ended badly. I hope they can tell her just that, because it is the truth, and that can never hurt her."

The social worker again reassured Don that he felt the couple who had adopted his little girl accepted the circumstances of her birth, felt understanding and sympathetic toward both of her natural parents, and would be quite comfortable in explaining this to the child as she grew up.

As for Don, the social worker suggested that seeking gratification through the little girl who had been placed for adoption would never be entirely satisfactory. It could only be second best to getting married and having children that he could help to raise. After all, a child is created simply by the meeting of a sperm and an egg, while parenthood is achieved by experiencing the heartaches, joys, pains, and pleasures of raising a child.

APPENDIX

Standardized Case Recording Form (SCRF)

The Standardized Case Recording Form (SCRF) was used to evaluate benefits in casework services to clients. The method originally devised as a research tool may be equally suited to case recording in its own right. Because SCRF and its content are based on experience, it can be revised easily and simply according to the needs of its users.

There is a need in casework to specify and isolate the effectiveness of casework method under varying situations and conditions. One method for helping to achieve this objective is that of recording specific results of cases as seen through the eyes of the worker. With more precise tools, based on practice, progress may be made in the attainment of this objective. The SCRF may be one step in this direction, particularly in the study of illegitimacy, but it has broader implications for the field.

Note: Section I pertains to case recording early in the casework process, while Section II pertains to case recording at the termination of the casework process. Insofar as possible, items are identical for both sections of SCRF. Through this system, changes occurring during casework can be documented and analyzed.

SCRF SECTION I - UNMARRIED FATHERS

Ident.________
Local________
Non-local______

This section of SCRF, composed of Parts A-F inclusive, is to be completed NO LATER THAN AT THE END OF THE THIRD INTERVIEW.

There will be many instances where you are asked to check an alternative that best describes your UF. In some instances you may not have discussed a point(s) specifically. However, you may have gained impressions about his attitudes or the attitudes of others through your casework relationship; such impressions may serve as a basis for your response throughout SCRF.

Number of interviews held prior to completion of this section of SCRF___

Worker ____________________

Date ____________

SCRF I - A, UF'S - CASEWORK GOALS

Please review the list of possible goals below, check one alternative for each possible goal, AS RELATED TO THIS CASE.

NOTE: List any additional goals under the heading provided.

	This is NOT a goal	This is a minor goal	This is a rather important goal	This is a most important goal
1. To involve the UF's parent(s) in a relationship with agency, (e.g., to bring parent(s) to VDM).				
2. To help UF to understand the factors in himself that led to unwed parenthood.				
3. To help UF to understand factors in others, (e.g., personality of UM, social factors, etc.) that led to unwed parenthood.				
4. To help UF to understand implicatons involved in bringing a new human being into the world.				
5. To help UF to behave responsibly in dealing with problems of unwed parenthood.				
6. To help UF to develop a realistic relationship (or termination of relationship with UM.				
7. To help UF to develop personality resources that will prevent him from again becoming an unwed father.				
8. To help the UF to maintain agency contact until the birth of the baby.				
9. To help the UF to be supportive and helpful to the UM during her pregnancy.				
10. To motivate the UF to participate in making the appropriate decision with respect to the baby's future.				
11. To help the UF in making the appropriate decision with respect to his own future.				
12. To motivate the UF to assume his share of the responsibility by making financial contributions for medical and maternity costs.				
13. To help the UF understand his rights and rights of the UM concerning decision-making with respect to the baby.				

14. Additional goals: ____

____

	Definitely	Probably	Probably not	Definitely not	Does not apply	Do not know
15. As it appears to me now, the UF should encourage the UM to keep her baby.						
16. As it appears to me now, the UF should encourage the UM to place her baby for adoption.						
17. As it appears to me now, the UF should encourage the UM to urge her parent(s) to keep the baby.						
18. As it appears to me now, the <u>UF</u> should keep the baby.						
19. As it appears to me now, the UF should encourage his parent(s) to keep the baby.						

20. Comments:

SCRF I - B, UF'S - UM - UF RELATIONSHIPS

Following are some statements concerning the relationships between the UM and UF. You are asked to read each statement and check the one alternative that most nearly describes the relationship between your UF and UM.

	Love	Friendship	Casual	Hostile
1. He described the relationship with the UM that existed prior to conception as				
2. He now considers the relationship to be				
3. He believes the UM regarded the relationship prior to conception as				
4. He believes the UM now considers the relationship to be				

	Definitely	Probably	Probably not	Definitely not	Does not apply	Do not know
5. In comparing the UM with himself, he believes she is superior to him.						
6. Prior to conception, he thought of the UM as a possible marriage partner.						
7. Does he believe the UM thought of him as a possible marriage partner prior to conception?						
8. He <u>now</u> thinks of UM in terms of a possible marriage partner.						
9. He believes the UM <u>now</u> thinks of him in terms of a possible marriage partner.						

10. Does he believe the UM's attitudes have changed toward him during her pregnancy?
    10-a. If no (to 10 above), is he disturbed because no change has taken place?

	Yes	No	Does not apply	Do not know
10.				
10-a.				

10-b. If yes (to 10 above), identify these attitudinal changes.

____

____

	Very	Some-what	Not very	Not at all	Does not apply	Do not know
11. How concerned does he feel the UM is about him and his welfare?						
12. How concerned does he feel the UM is about what happens to the baby?						

	Yes	No
13. Do you see serious problems in the current relationship between the UF and UM?		

13-a. If you answered yes (to 13 above), please briefly describe these problems:

SCRF I - C, UF'S - ATTITUDES OF UF'S PARENTS

For each statement below, check the one alternative that applies:	Yes	No	Does not apply
1. UF's mother is available for agency contact (alive, in greater L.A. area).			
2. Worker made an effort to involve UF's mother.			
3. Mother was involved by agency (was seen, interviewed, etc.)			
4. UF's father is available for agency contact (alive, in greater L.A. area).			
5. Worker made an effort to involve UF's father.			
6. Father was involved by agency (was seen, interviewed, etc.)			

For the statements below, circle the appropriate response: (approximations acceptable).

7. Number of personal contacts of worker with mother. None-1-2-3-4-over 5
8. Number of phone contacts of worker with mother. None-1-2-3-4-over 5
9. Number of personal contacts of worker with father. None-1-2-3-4-over 5
10. Number of phone contacts of worker with father. None-1-2-3-4-over 5

Statements about attitudes of parents of UF follow. Each parent is treated separately. (M designates mother; F designates father.)

For statements below, check the one alternative that applies:

		F	M
11. Concern with legal implications	a. extremely	___	___
	b. very	___	___
	c. somewhat	___	___
	d. not at all	___	___
	e. don't know	___	___
	f. does not apply	___	___
12. Concern with what other people (neighbors, relatives, etc.) might think of them as parents.	a. extremely	___	___
	b. very	___	___
	c. somewhat	___	___
	d. not at all	___	___
	e. don't know	___	___
	f. does not apply	___	___
13. Concern with what other people (neighbors, relatives, etc.) will think of their son in view of his involvement in an out of wedlock pregnancy.	a. extremely	___	___
	b. very	___	___
	c. somewhat	___	___
	d. not at all	___	___
	e. don't know	___	___
	f. does not apply	___	___

		F	M
14. Fear of possibilities (real or imagined) that son will be (pushed) (urged) (plunged) into marriage.	a. extremely	___	___
	b. very	___	___
	c. somewhat	___	___
	d. not at all	___	___
	e. don't know	___	___
	f. does not apply	___	___
15. Concern with how soon a marriage can be arranged.	a. extremely	___	___
	b. very	___	___
	c. somewhat	___	___
	d. not at all	___	___
	e. don't know	___	___
	f. does not apply	___	___
16. Concern with arrangements for UM's care, medical, maternity home.	a. extremely	___	___
	b. very	___	___
	c. somewhat	___	___
	d. not at all	___	___
	e. don't know	___	___
	f. does not apply	___	___
17. Concern with getting financial help from UM (or her family) to meet maternity expense.	a. extremely	___	___
	b. very	___	___
	c. somewhat	___	___
	d. not at all	___	___
	e. don't know	___	___
	f. does not apply	___	___
18. Concern with ways in which to punish UF.	a. extremely	___	___
	b. very	___	___
	c. somewhat	___	___
	d. not at all	___	___
	e. don't know	___	___
	f. does not apply	___	___
19. Critical of self concerning own role in relations to son (degree of interest taken in son's social life, partner, sex education, etc.)	a. extremely	___	___
	b. very	___	___
	c. somewhat	___	___
	d. not at all	___	___
	e. don't know	___	___
	f. does not apply	___	___
20. Supportive of agency plan to involve the UF.	a. extremely	___	___
	b. very	___	___
	c. somewhat	___	___
	d. not at all	___	___
	e. don't know	___	___
	f. does not apply	___	___
21. Supportive of son.	a. extremely	___	___
	b. very	___	___
	c. somewhat	___	___
	d. not at all	___	___
	e. don't know	___	___
	f. does not apply	___	___

SCRF I - D, UF'S - DECISION MAKING

Following are some statements concerning the decision-making process in plans for the baby AND self. You are asked to read each statement and select the one alternative that most nearly describes your unwed mother.

	Definitely	Probably	Probably not	Definitely not	Does not apply	Do not know
1. UF desires UM to keep her baby.						
2. UF believes adoption is best solution.						
3. UF expects that UM's parents will care for baby.						
4. UF expects that other relatives of UM will care for baby.						
5. UF expects to care for baby.						
6. UF expects his parent(s) to care for baby.						
7. UF expects that he and UM will marry soon.						
8. UF expects that he and another woman (not UM) will marry soon.						
For Items 9-11 inclusive, a 7th category is added, viz., "Is Not Aware of Proposed Decision." (Check first column for this.)						
9. UF's mother approves of UF's proposed decision.						
10. UF's father approves of UF's proposed decision.						
11. UM approves of UF's proposed decision.						
12. UF sees value in exploring various alternatives concerning plans for baby.						
13. UF is interested in having his mother participate in decision-making process.						
14. UF is interested in having his father participate in the decision-making process.						
15. UF raised issue concerning need and/or advisability of his contributing financially.						
16. Caseworker raised issue concerning need and/or advisability of UF contributing financially.						
17. As his social worker I believe that UF's suggested plan for the baby is realistic and appropriate.						
18. As his social worker, I believe that UF's current plan for SELF is realistic and appropriate.						

19. State briefly any crucial issues concerning the decision-making process you plan to explore with the UF and/or his parent(s).

SCRF I - E, UF'S - ATTITUDES

Following is a series of statements that have been used to describe some of the feelings and beliefs of unwed fathers.

You are asked to review each statement and determine the degree to which each describes your UF, using the following scale:

A: I agree very much
B: I agree pretty much
C: I agree a little
D: I disagree a little
E: I disagree pretty much
F: I disagree very much
G: does not apply
H: do not know

Mark each statement in the left margin according to how much you agree.

____ 1. UF indicates he entered into sexual act with full knowledge of potential outcome - i.e., pregnancy.
____ 2. UF did not use or urge partner to use contraceptives because he did not seriously believe UM might become pregnant.
____ 3. UF views his involvement in the pregnancy as something that will materially effect his future.
____ 4. UF believes that UM's pregnancy will bind his partner to him forever.
____ 5. UF tends to see pregnancy as a way of gaining parental love and appreciation.
____ 6. UF tends to view agency as source that will magically solve all his problems.
____ 7. UF talks in terms of UM keeping her baby, yet knows she is inadequate because of her youth or personal characteristics to properly raise a child.
____ 8. UF believes he can continue the relationship with the UM as though nothing has happened.
____ 9. UF tends to regard pregnancy as an isolated happening that will have little or no effect on his relationships with his parent(s).
____ 10. UF takes the attitude that if UM keeps her baby he will ultimately marry her.
____ 11. UF sees baby as a potential "gift" to his parent(s).
____ 12. UF views pregnancy as something that nature wills and that he cannot control.
____ 13. UF believes that he is UM's "one and only" love.
____ 14. UF has good insight into himself; he understands his personal weaknesses and strengths.
____ 15. UF is deeply concerned about the child's future.
____ 16. UF is genuinely undisturbed by the fact that he is an unwed parent.
____ 17. UF has strong guilt feelings.
____ 18. UF blames his partner for her situation.
____ 19. UF is dependent upon his mother for most of his decisions.
____ 20. UF regards pregnancy as something that "just happened."
____ 21. UF feels rejected by the UM.
____ 22. UF sees baby as an instrument to hurt his parent(s).
____ 23. UF has a history of deliquent behavior in addition to being an unwed father.
____ 24. UF understands the reason for agency involvement.
____ 25. UF feels rejected by his peers.
____ 26. UF is concerned about the consequences of pregnancy to himself.
____ 27. UF tends to view pregnancy as something that will go away.
____ 28. UF tends to view sexual relations as proof of partner's (UM's) love.
____ 29. UF believes that entering into sexual relations proves he is a man.

____30. UF tends to regard the baby as something apart from his feelings and self.
____31. UF gets along well with his mother.
____32. UF desires UM to retain her baby - plan realistic.
____33. UF is pleased at being able to impregnate.
____34. UF has a cooperative feeling toward the agency.
____35. UF views marriage as the best solution to his problem.
____36. UF sees his experience as one that will change his sexual pattern.
____37. UF accepts the idea that he has some responsibility for participating in decision-making.
____38. UF is taking the matter of pregnancy rather lightly.
____39. UF never wants to see his partner (UM) again.
____40. UF regards himself as the nearly "perfect man" who can do little or not wrong.
____41. Attitudes and behavior of UF suggest that "he would do it all over again" with the UM if circumstances were generally similar.
____42. UF has known UM long enough to form a realistic impression of what she really is like.
____43. UF believes that the sexual act that led to his pregnancy was an emotional spur-of-the-moment event.
____44. UF sees nothing wrong in conceiving a child out of wedlock.
____45. UF feels rejected by his mother.
____46. UF is concerned about consequences to his partner (UM).
____47. UF is dependent upon the caseworker for most of his decision.
____48. UF blames himself for his situation.
____49. UF has romantic notions about his partner (the UM).
____50. UF sees the experience as one that will change his life in a negative fashion.
____51. UF is concerned principally with the past - with what "has been."
____52. UF believes that engaging in the sexual act is <u>not</u> to be equated with love.
____53. UF has good understanding of male and female sexual anatomy and function.
____54. UF regards UM as the nearly "perfect woman" who can do no wrong.
____55. UF sees baby as an instrument being used by UM to hurt him.
____56. UF feels rejected by his father.
____57. UF has a cooperative feeling toward the worker.
____58. UF refuses to face his situation.
____59. UF desires his parent(s) to retain baby - plan unrealistic.
____60. If working, UF functions well on the job.
____61. UF blames other people - such as his parent(s) - for his situation.
____62. UF expects sexual relations to be a consistently ethereal, "moonlight and roses" kind of experience.
____63. UF deals primarily with the present - with the "here-and-now."
____64. UF sees the UM as a kind of "shadow figure," without much of an identity as a human being.
____65. UF expresses hate toward his partner (UM).
____66. UF sees experience as one that will change his life in a positive fashion.
____67. UF expresses hate toward his parent(s).
____68. If a student, UF functions well as a student.
____69. UF has a good understanding of UM as a person with personality weaknesses and strengths.
____70. UF sees his experience as one that changes his choice of a future partner.
____71. UF is facing his problem realistically.

72. Describe in some detail the specific fantasy notions (if any) held by UF and any changes that have taken place during the casework process.
73. Describe attitudes or behaviors most characteristic of the UF and any changes that have taken place during the casework process.

SCRF I - F, UF'S - INVOLVEMENT OF THE UF

Following are some statements concerning attitudes of the UF and others toward his involvement in the casework process and assertive casework methods used to effect involvement.

Note that each statement contains parts a, b, and c; each of which is answered by checking the alternative that applies.

	Strongly refused in-volve-ment of UF	Refused involve-ment but "door left open"	Reluc-tantly agreed to UF's in-volve-ment	Read-ily agreed to UF's in-volve-ment	Person-ally ini-tiated plans for UF's involve-ment	Does not apply	Do not know
1. The UF's reaction toward involvement was:							
a. at first contact (prior to first interview).							
b. during first interview.							
c. during later interviews (but no later than third interview).							
2. The UM's reaction toward UF's involvement was:							
a. at first contact (prior to first interview).							
b. during first interview.							
c. during later interviews (but no later than third interview).							

	Strongly refused involvement of UF	Refused involvement but "door left open"	Reluctantly agreed to UF's involvement	Readily agreed to UF's involvement	Personally initiated plans for UF's involvement	Does not apply	Do not know
3. The UF's <u>father's</u> reaction toward UF's involvement was: a. at first contact (prior to first interview).							
b. during <u>first</u> interview.							
c. during later interviews (but no later than third interview).							
4. The UF's <u>mother's</u> reaction toward UF's involvement was: a. at first contact (prior to first interview).							
b. during <u>first</u> interview.							
c. during later interviews (but no later than third interview).							
5. The <u>UM's</u> <u>mother's</u> action toward UF's involvement was: a. at first contact (prior to first interview).							
b. during <u>first</u> interview.							
c. during later interviews (but no later than third interview).							
6. The <u>UM's</u> <u>father's</u> reaction toward UF's involvement was: a. at first contact (prior to first interview).							
b. during <u>first</u> interview.							
c. during later interviews (but no later than third interview).							

	This method was NOT used	This method was used to a slight degree	This method was used to some degree	This method was used to a strong degree	Does not apply
7. Male worker voiced expectation to UF that UF should participate.					
8. Male worker voiced expectation to UF that UF must participate.					
9. Male worker took a positive stand with UF's parent(s) that UF should participate.					
10. Male worker took a positive stand with UF's parent(s) that UF must participate.					
11. Female worker voiced expectation with UM that UF should participate.					
12. Female worker voiced expectation with UM that UF must participate.					
13. Female worker voiced expectation with UM's parent(s) that UF should participate.					
14. Female worker voiced expectation with UM's parent(s) that UF must participate.					
15. Male worker suggested to UF that serious legal consequences could result if he fails to participate.					
16. Male worker suggested to UF's parent(s) that serious legal consequences could result if UF fails to participate.					
17. Male worker enlisted the aid of other local agencies (e.g. law enforcement) to help facilitate UF's participation.					

17-a. If above method used, list agency(s) used.

____

18. Male worker urged participation on basis that UF has a social responsibility for the welfare of the unborn child.					
19. Male worker urged participation on basis that UF has a social responsibility for the welfare of his partner (UM).					
20. Male worker urged participation on basis of UF's responsibility to see UM through a most difficult situation.					

	This method was NOT used	This method was used to a slight degree	This method was used to some degree	This method was used to a strong degree	Does not apply
21. Male worker urged participation on basis of what such participation will mean to UF in his personal growth.					
22. Male worker urged participation on basis of importance participation can have on UM in making a sound decision re disposition of baby.					
23. Male worker urged participation on basis of importance of such participation in helping him assess his past, current, and future relationships with UM.					

24. Other methods used:

25. How many phone calls did the worker have with the UF before he agreed to become involved? (circle). 1 2 3 4 5 over 5

26. How many letter did the worker send to the UF before he agreed to become involved? 1 2 3 4 5 over 5

27. How many phone calls did the worker have with persons other than UF (UF's parents, relatives, etc.) before the UF agreed to become involved? (circle) 1 2 3 4 5 over 5

28. How many letters did the worker send to persons other than UF (UF's parents, relatives, etc.) before the UF agreed to become involved? (circle) 1 2 3 4 5 over 5

29. Comment briefly on:
    a. What you consider to have been the most successful assertive methods used in this case;
    b. your assessment of the reasons why these methods were successful;
    c. what you consider to have been unsuccessful assertive methods used in this case;
    d. your assessment of the reasons why these methods were unsuccessful.

SCRF SECTION II - UNMARRIED FATHERS

Ident.________
Local________
Non-local______

This section of SCRF, composed of Parts R - X inclusive, is to be completed at termination.

There will be many instances where you are asked to check an alternative that best describes your UF. In some instances you may not have discussed a point(s) specifically. However, you may have gained impressions about his attitude or the attitudes of others through your casework relationships; such impressions may serve as a basis for your response throughout SCRF.

Number of interviews held prior to completion of this section of SCRF___

Worker ______________________

Date ____________

SCRF II - R, UF'S - CASEWORK GOALS

Please review the list of possible goals below. Check one alternative for each possible goal, AS RELATED TO THIS CASE.

NOTE: List any additional goals under the heading provided.

	This never was a goal	This goal definitely NOT reached	This goal reached to a minor degree	This goal reached to some extent	This goal definitely reached
1. To involve UF's parent(s) in a relationship with agency (e.g., to bring parent(s) to Vista Del Mar).					
2. To help UF to understand the factors in himself that led to unwed parenthood.					
3. To help UF to understand factors in others, (e.g., personality of UM, social factors, etc.) that led to unwed parenthood.					
4. To help UF to understand implications involved in bringing a new human being into the world.					
5. To help UF to behave responsibly in dealing with problems of unwed parenthood.					
6. To help UF to develop a realistic relationship (or termination of relationship) with UM.					
7. To help UF to develop personality resources that will prevent him from again becoming an unwed father.					
8. To help the UF to maintain agency contact until the birth of the baby.					

	This never was a goal	This goal definitely NOT reached	This goal reached to a minor degree	This goal reached to some extent	This goal definitely reached
9. To help the UF to be supportive and helpful to the UM during her pregnancy.					
10. To motivate the UF to participate in making the appropriate decision with respect to the baby's future.					
11. To help the UF im making the appropriate decision with respect to his own future.					
12. To motivate the UF to assume his share of the responsibility by making financial contributions for medical and maternity costs.					
13. To help the UF understand his rights and rights of UM concerning decision-making with respect to the baby.					

14. Additional goals:

____

____

	Definitely	Probably	Probably not	Definitely not	Does not apply	Do not know
15. As it appears to me now, the UF should encourage the UM to keep her baby.						
16. As it appears to me now, the UF should encourage the UM to place her baby for adoption.						
17. As it appears to me now, the UF should encourage the UM to urge her parent(s) to keep the baby.						
18. As it appears to me now, the UF should keep the baby.						
19. As it appears to me now, the UF should encourage his parent(s) to keep the baby.						

20. Please write a short statement of your views as to what might have been done to prevent this UF from becoming an unwed parent.
21. Please indicate whether, and if so how, your objectives for the UF changed during the casework process.
22. Comments.

SCRF II - S, UF'S - UM-UF RELATIONSHIPS

Following are some statements concerning the relationships between the UM and UF. You are asked to read each statement and check the one alternative that most nearly describes the relationship between your UF and the UM.

	Love	Friendship	Casual	Hostile
1. UF described the relationship with the UM that existed prior to conception as:				
2. UF now considers the relationship to be:				
3. UF believes the UM regarded the relationship prior to conception as:				
4. UF believes the UM now considers the relationship to be:				

	Definitely	Probably	Probably not	Definitely not	Does not apply	Do not know
5. In comparing the UM with himself, UF believes she is superior to him.						
6. Prior to conception, UF thought of the UM as a possible marriage partner.						
7. Does UF believe the UM thought of him as a possible marriage partner prior to conception?						
8. UF now thinks of UM in terms of a possible marriage partner.						
9. UF believes the UM now thinks of him in terms of a possible marriage partner.						

	Yes	No	Does not apply	Does not know
10. Does UF believe the UM's attitudes have changed toward him during her pregnancy?				
10-a. If no (to 10 above), is UF disturbed because no change has taken place?				

10-b. If yes (to 10 above), identify these attitudinal changes:

____

____

____

	Very	Some-what	Not very	Not at all	Does not apply	Do not know
11. How concerned does UF feel the UM is about him and his welfare?						
12. How concerned does he feel the UM is about what happens to the baby?						

	Yes	No
13. Do you see serious problems in the current relationship between the UF and UM?		

13-a. If you answered yes (to 13 above), please briefly describe these problems.

13-b. If you answered yes (to 13 above), what action have you taken to help the UF resolve these problems?

13-c. If you answered no (to 13 above), and this represents a change during the casework process, please assess reasons for these changes, including the effects of casework intervention.

SCRF II - T, UF'S - ATTITUDES OF UF'S PARENTS

For each statement below, check the one alternative that applies:	Yes	No	Does not apply
1. UF's mother is available for agency contact (alive, in greater L.A. area).			
2. Worker made an effort to involve UF's mother.			
3. Mother was involved by agency (was seen, interviewed, etc.)			
4. UF's father is available for agency contact (alive, in greater L.A. area).			
5. Worker made an effort to involve UF's father.			
6. Father was involved by agency (was seen, interviewed, etc.)			

For the statements below, circle the appropriate response: (approximations acceptable).

7. Number of personal contacts of worker with mother. None-1-2-3-4-over 5
8. Number of phone contacts of worker with mother. None-1-2-3-4-over 5
9. Number of personal contacts of worker with father. None-1-2-3-4-over 5
10. Number of phone contacts of worker with father. None-1-2-3-4-over 5

Statements about attitudes of parents of UF follow. Each parent is treated separately. (M designates mother; F designates father.)

For statements below, check the one alternative that applies: F M

11. Concern with legal implications
a. extremely ___ ___
b. very ___ ___
c. somewhat ___ ___
d. not at all ___ ___
e. don't know ___ ___
f. does not apply ___ ___

12. Concern with what other people (neighbors, relatives, etc.) might think of them as parents.
a. extremely ___ ___
b. very ___ ___
c. somewhat ___ ___
d. not at all ___ ___
e. don't know ___ ___
f. does not apply ___ ___

13. Concern with what other people (neighbors, relatives, etc.) will think of their son in view of his involvement in an out of wedlock pregnancy.
a. extremely ___ ___
b. very ___ ___
c. somewhat ___ ___
d. not at all ___ ___
e. don't know ___ ___
f. does not apply ___ ___

		F	M
14. Fear of possibilities (real or imagined) that son will be (pushed) (urged) (plunged) into marriage.	a. extremely	___	___
	b. very	___	___
	c. somewhat	___	___
	d. not at all	___	___
	e. don't know	___	___
	f. does not apply	___	___
15. Concern with how soon a marriage can be arranged.	a. extremely	___	___
	b. very	___	___
	c. somewhat	___	___
	d. not at all	___	___
	e. don't know	___	___
	f. does not apply	___	___
16. Concern with arrangements for UM's care, medical, maternity home.	a. extremely	___	___
	b. very	___	___
	c. somewhat	___	___
	d. not at all	___	___
	e. don't know	___	___
	f. does not apply	___	___
17. Concern with getting financial help from UM (or her family) to meet maternity expense.	a. extremely	___	___
	b. very	___	___
	c. somewhat	___	___
	d. not at all	___	___
	e. don't know	___	___
	f. does not apply	___	___
18. Concern with ways in which to punish UF.	a. extremely	___	___
	b. very	___	___
	c. somewhat	___	___
	d. not at all	___	___
	e. don't know	___	___
	f. does not apply	___	___
19. Critical of self concerning own role in relations to son (degree of interest taken in son's social life, partner, sex education, etc.)	a. extremely	___	___
	b. very	___	___
	c. somewhat	___	___
	d. not at all	___	___
	e. don't know	___	___
	f. does not apply	___	___
20. Supportive of agency plan to involve the UF.	a. extremely	___	___
	b. very	___	___
	c. somewhat	___	___
	d. not at all	___	___
	e. don't know	___	___
	f. does not apply	___	___
21. Supportive of son.	a. extremely	___	___
	b. very	___	___
	c. somewhat	___	___
	d. not at all	___	___
	e. don't know	___	___
	f. does not apply	___	___

SCRF - II - U, UF'S - DECISION MAKING

Following are some statements concerning the decision-making process as it concerns UF's participation and plans for SELF. You are asked to read each statement and select the one alternative that most nearly describes your unwed father.

NOTE: SOME ITEMS ASK FOR A SHORT NARRATIVE.

	Definitely	Probably	Probably not	Definitely not	Does not apply	Do not know
1. UM kept baby in an out of wedlock status.						
2. UM kept her baby and married.						
3. UM has placed baby for adoption.						
4. UF expects that he and UM will marry soon.						
5. UF has married UM.						
6. UF's intimate relationship with UM has terminated.						
7. UF expects that he and another woman (not UM) will marry soon.						
8. UF has married another woman (not UM).						
9. UF is caring for baby.						
10. UF's parent(s) are caring for baby.						
11. Other relatives of the UF are caring for baby.						
12. UF explored the various alternatives concerning plans for the baby.						
13. UF explored various alternatives concerning plans for self.						
14. UF's participation in the decision-making process helped to bring about a good decision re disposition of the baby.						
15. UF's participation in the decision-making process helped to bring about a poor decision re disposition of the baby.						
16. Participation in the decision-making process had little or not meaning to the UF.						
17. Participation in the decision-making process actually had little or no meaning to the UM.						
18. UM consistently excluded UF from active participation in the decision-making re plans for the baby.						
19. UF participated financially.						
20. UF's mother's participation in the decision-making process was a vital force in determining the UM's final act - i.e., disposition of the baby.						

	Definitely	Probably	Probably not	Definitely not	Does not apply	Do not know	Is not aware of UM's decision
21. UF's mother approves final decision.							
22. UF's father approves final decision.							
23. UF approves final decision.							

PLEASE EXPLAIN IN SOME DETAIL.

	Definitely	Probably	Probably not	Definitely not	Does not apply	Do not know
24. UF's father's participation in the decision-making process was a vital force in determining the UM's final act - i.e., disposition of the baby.						
PLEASE EXPLAIN IN SOME DETAIL.						
25. UF's participation in the decision-making process was a vital force in determining the UM's final act - i.e., disposition of the baby.						
PLEASE EXPLAIN IN SOME DETAIL.						
26. As his social worker, I believe UF's final suggested plan for the baby is realistic and appropriate.						
27. As his social worker, I believe UF's final plan for self is realistic and appropriate.						

28. State briefly significant dynamics that occurred during the decision-making process, paying particular attention to:
    (a) dynamics that had a positive effect: and
    (b) dynamics that had a negative effect.

SCRF II - V, UF'S - INVOLVEMENT OF UF

	Yes	No
1. The UF, while originally "not to be seen," needed to be seen ("exception").		
2. The UF lives outside the L.A. area.		
3. The UF was "to be seen" and was seen.		

4. How many personal interviews were held with the UF? (circle) 1 2 3 4 5 6 7 8 9 10 other__
5. How many phoned interviews were held with the UF? (circle) 1 2 3 4 5 6 7 8 9 10 other__
6. How many letters were sent to the UF during the casework process (other than routine letters, such as confirming appointments)? 1 2 3 4 5 6 7 8 9 10 other__

FOR STATEMENTS BELOW, CHECK THE ONE ALTERNATIVE THAT APPLIES.

	Strongly refused involvement of UF	Refused involvement but "door left open"	Reluctantly agreed to UF's involvement	Readily agreed to UF's involve ment	Personally initiated plans for UF's involvement	Does not apply	Do not know
7. The UF's reaction toward involvement at the end of casework was:							
8. The UM's reaction towards UF's involvement at the end of casework:							
9. The UF's father's reaction toward UF's involvement at the end of casework was:							
10. The UF's mother's reaction toward UF's involvement at the end of casework was:							
11. The UM's mother's reaction towards UF's involvement at the end was:							
12. The UM's father's reaction towards UF's involvement at the end was:							

	Definitely	Probably	Probably not	Definitely not	Does not apply	Do not know
13. In general, the UF participated because he felt he must.						
14. In general, the UF participated because he felt he should.						

	Definitely	Probably	Probably not	Definitely not	Does not apply	Do not know
15. In general, the UF participated because he wanted to.						
16. In general, UF saw little or no reason for his participation.						
17. In general, the UF kept appointments only because the worker consistently reminded, urged, insisted.						
18. In general, the UF kept appointments only because of parental pressure.						
19. In general, the UF kept appointments only because of outside pressures, (e.g., law enforcement.)						

19-a. List any such agency:

____

____

20. In general, the UF kept appointments only because of pressures by the UM.						
21. In general, the UF kept appointments only because of pressures by UM's parents.						
22. In general, the UF kept appointments as a method to reduce possibility of legal sanctions.						
23. In general, the UF kept appointments as a way of meeting agency expectations.						
24. In general, the UF kept appointments because he felt results would be helpful to the UM.						
25. In general, the UF kept appointments because he felt results would be helpful to himself.						

26. Comment briefly on:

a. The extent to which it was necessary to continue assertive methods once the UF became involved with the agency.

b. General reactions of UF to assertive methods (if used).

c. General reactions of his parent(s) to assertive methods (if used). Specify parent(s).

d. Your assessment of whether the UF would have become involved with the agency if assertive methods had <u>not</u> been employed.

e. Your assessment of whether the UF would have become involved with the UM in decision-making, etc., if assertive methods had <u>not</u> been employed.

SCRF II - W, UF'S - FINANCIAL CONTRIBUTIONS

Following are some statements concerning attitudes of UF regarding contributions, and worker action in bringing about UF's decision to contribute. Check one alternative for each item.

	Yes	No	Does not apply
1. The caseworker was instrumental in raising the issue of UF's responsibility in contributing financially.			
If yes (to 1 above):			
1-a. Worker indicated UF must contribute.			
1-b. Worker indicated UF should contribute.			
1-c. Worker suggested a specific sum or percent of total cost.			
2. The UF volunteered that he wanted to make a financial contribution.			
3. The worker enlisted the help of UF's parent(s) to bring about financial participation of the UF.			
4. The worker enlisted the help of the UM to bring about financial participation of the UF.			
5. The worker enlisted the help of UM's parent(s) to bring about financial participation of the UF.			
6. The UF agreed to the concept of contributing and agreed to contribute.			
7. The UF agreed to the concept of contributing financially but stated he could not contribute.			
If yes to 7 above: 7-a. Worker agrees that UF's assessment of inability to participate is reasonable and realistic.			
8. The UF disagreed with the concept of contributing, but agreed to contribute even though he disagreed in principle.			

9. Other methods used: ____________________

____

____

PAYMENT RECORD

Amount agreed upon, $__________

DATE	AMOUNT PAID	TO WHOM PAID
______	______	______
______	______	______
______	______	______
______	______	______

TOTAL: __________

AMOUNT TO BE PAID: __________ BALANCE: __________

SCRF II - X, UF'S - ATTITUDES

Following is a series of statements that have been used to describe some of the feelings and beliefs of unwed fathers.

You are asked to review each statement and determine the degree to which each describes your UF, using the following scale:

A: I agree very much
B: I agree pretty much
C: I agree a little
D: I disagree a little
E: I disagree pretty much
F: I disagree very much
G: does not apply
H: do not know

Mark each statement in the left margin according to how much you agree.

____ 1. UF indicates he entered into sexual act with full knowledge of potential outcome - i.e., pregnancy.
____ 2. UF did not use or urge partner to use contraceptives because he did not seriously believe UM might become pregnant.
____ 3. UF views his involvement in the pregnancy as something that will materially effect his future.
____ 4. UF believes that UM's pregnancy will bind his partner to him forever.
____ 5. UF tends to see pregnancy as a way of gaining parental love and appreciation.
____ 6. UF tends to view agency as source that will magically solve all his problems.
____ 7. UF talks in terms of UM keeping her baby, yet knows she is inadequate because of her youth or personal characteristics to properly raise a child.
____ 8. UF believes he can continue the relationship with the UM as though nothing has happened.
____ 9. UF tends to regard pregnancy as an isolated happening that will have little or no effect on his relationships with his parent(s).
____ 10. UF takes the attitude that if UM keeps her baby he will ultimately marry her.
____ 11. UF sees baby as a potential "gift" to his parent(s).
____ 12. UF views pregnancy as something that nature wills and that he cannot control.
____ 13. UF believes that he is UM's "one and only" love.
____ 14. UF has good insight into himself: he understands his personal weaknesses and strengths.
____ 15. UF is deeply concerned about the child's future.
____ 16. UF is genuinely undisturbed by the fact that he is an unwed parent.
____ 17. UF has strong guilt feelings.
____ 18. UF blames his partner for her situation.
____ 19. UF is dependent upon his mother for most of his decisions.
____ 20. UF regards pregnancy as something that "just happened."
____ 21. UF feels rejected by the UM.
____ 22. UF sees baby as an instrument to hurt his parent(s).
____ 23. UF has a history of deliquent behavior in addition to being an unwed father.
____ 24. UF understands the reason for agency involvement.
____ 25. UF feels rejected by his peers.
____ 26. UF is concerned about the consequences of pregnancy to himself.
____ 27. UF tends to view pregnancy as something that will go away.
____ 28. UF tends to view sexual relations as proof of partner's (UM's) love.

____29. UF believes that entering into sexual relations proves he is a man.
____30. UF tends to regard the baby as something apart from his feelings and self.
____31. UF gets along well with his mother.
____32. UF desires UM to retain her baby - plan realistic.
____33. UF is pleased at being able to impregnate.
____34. UF has a cooperative feeling toward the agency.
____35. UF views marriage as the best solution to his problem.
____36. UF sees his experience as one that will change his sexual pattern.
____37. UF accepts the idea that he has some responsibility for participating in decision-making.
____38. UF is taking the matter of pregnancy rather lightly.
____39. UF never wants to see his partner (UM) again.
____40. UF regards himself as the nearly "perfect man" who can do little or not wrong.
____41. Attitudes and behavior of UF suggest that "he would do it all over again" with the UM if circumstances were generally similar.
____42. UF has known UM long enough to form a realistic impression of what she really is like.
____43. UF believes that the sexual act that led to his pregnancy was an emotional spur-of-the-moment event.
____44. UF sees nothing wrong in conceiving a child out of wedlock.
____45. UF feels rejected by his mother.
____46. UF is concerned about consequences to his partner (UM).
____47. UF is dependent upon the caseworker for most of his decision.
____48. UF blames himself for his situation.
____49. UF has romantic notions about his partner (the UM).
____50. UF sees the experience as one that will change his life in a negative fashion.
____51. UF is concerned principally with the past - with what "has been.
____52. UF believes that engaging in the sexual act is <u>not</u> to be equated with love.
____53. UF has good understanding of male and female sexual anatomy and function.
____54. UF regards UM as the nearly "perfect woman" who can do no wrong.
____55. UF sees baby as an instrument being used by UM to hurt him.
____56. UF feels rejected by his father.
____57. UF has a cooperative feeling toward the worker.
____58. UF refuses to face his situation.
____59. UF desires his parent(s) to retain baby - plan unrealistic.
____60. If working, UF functions well on the job.
____61. UF blames other people - such as his parent(s) - for his situation.
____62. UF expects sexual relations to be a consistently ethereal, "moonlight and roses" kind of experience.
____63. UF deals primarily with the present - with the "here-and-now."
____64. UF sees the UM as a kind of "shadow figure," without much of an identity as a human being.
____65. UF expresses hate toward his partner (UM).
____66. UF sees experience as one that will change his life in a positive fashion.
____67. UF expresses hate toward his parent(s).
____68. If a student, UF functions well as a student.
____69. UF has a good understanding of UM as a person with personality weaknesses and strengths.
____70. UF sees his experience as one that changes his choice of a future partner.

__71. UF is facing his problem realistically.

72. Describe in some detail the specific fantasy notions (if any) held by UF and any changes that have taken place during the casework process.

73. Describe attitudes or behaviors most characteristic of the UF and any changes that have taken place during the casework process.

Author Index

Anglim, Elizabeth, 14
Chaskel, Ruth, 13
Deschin, Cecia S., 25-26, 31
Erikson, Erik H., 25, 26, 30, 31, 117, 119, 122
Evans, Byron W., 62, 155
Furie, Sidney, 155
Futterman, Samuel, 149, 155
Gershenson, Charles, 19
Gough, Harrison G., 119, 121, 122
Grayson, Ellis S., 20
Hollingshead, August B., 36, 43
Hyman, Herbert, 62
Jessor, Richard, 27, 110-113, 114-116, 121,122
Livermore, Jean B., 149, 155
Pannor, Reuben, 62, 146, 155
Perkins, Robert F., 20
Pollack, Otto, 150, 155
Rapoport, Lydia, 146
Richmond, Mary, 139
Rowan, Matile, 146
Rubinstein, Elaine, 19
Sarnoff, Irving, 122
Sauber, Mignon, 19
Vincent, Clark E., 29, 30, 108-109, 122, 126, 134
Wedemeyer, J. M., 43
Wolins, Martin, 23, 30

Subject Index

Abortions, 84, 97
Achievement potential, 102, 108
Adoption, 13, 14-15, 26, 39, 42
Ages:
  differentials of unmarried "couples," 35
  unmarried fathers, 33-35
  unmarried mothers, 32-33
Aggressor, unwed mother as, 67, 120
Alienation, 75, 83, 114-115, 121
Approaches used by social workers, 54-59, 135-139
  affirmative, 137-139
  assertive, 55-56
  basic premises, 135-138
  constructive, 137
  motivational, 56, 58
Approval by others, 121
Background of unwed parents, 97-102
  education, 98
  marital status, 101
  parental origins, 101-102
  previous pregnancies, 101
  religion, 98-100
  social class, 98
Births, number of illegitimate, 11
California Psychological Inventory, 27, 103, 108, 110, 111, 114, 119, 147
California statistics, 33-35
Caseworkers *see* Social workers
Characteristics of unmarried fathers, 18
  age, 33-35
  personality, 102-122
  recidivism, 42-43
Child born out of wedlock
  decisions concerning future *see* Decisions about child's future
  legal rights, 12
  seen and handled by parents, 83, 152
  support of, 1, 93-96
Child Welfare League of America
  Standards for Services to Unmarried Parents, 17, 19
Children's Bureau (HEW), 17
Consequences of act, lack of concern for, 67, 70, 73
Constellations, family, 107, 122, 126
Contraceptives:
  knowledge of, 13, 70-73, 80, 120, 142
  education about, 142, 147, 153-154
  obtaining, 71, 72
  prior experience with, 71
Control groups, 22-24
  decision as to future of child, 85-87
  exceptions to, 63
  reaching unmarried fathers, 60, 63

Counseling services, 17, 75-83
in decision-making, 86-87, 91
group, 153
unmarried father, 75-83
unmarried mother, 77
Data collection, 10, 24-27
Decisions concerning child's future, 28, 82-83, 84-98
adoption, 82-83, 84, 86-87, 88
alternative solutions, 84-98, 124
child kept by father, 84
control groups, 86-87
effect of counseling, 86-87, 91
effect on parents, 82-84
financial support, 1, 93-96
foster home care, 84
involvement of father in, 85-87, 90-96
keeping baby, 82, 84, 86, 88
learning to live with, 86
legal rights of mother, 124
made by mothers, 86-87
marriage, 82, 84, 92
role of agency, 85-87
role of parents, 124-125
support of father, 90-96
Defensiveness, 107
Demonstration project, 17-19
study plan, 21-31
Despair, inner, 120-121
Deviants, social, 110-111
attitudes toward, 114-116, 121
personal disjunctions, 110-113
measurement of, 111-113
Education of unmarried parents, 37-38, 98
Ego identity, 117-118
"*Experiences of the Unwed Mother as a Parent*," 18, 19
Family Centered Project of St. Paul Minn., 56
Family constellations, 107, 122, 126
Family life programs, 154
Family relationships, 27-28, 77-78
conflict between parents, 117
home environment, 116
parental origins, 101-102
Family welfare services, 17
Fantasy orientation, 120, 121
Father of unwed father, 125-128
attitude of, 16
Femininity, 109, 118, 149
Financial support, 1, 93-96
Foster home care, 84
Frustration, 9-10
"Fun morality," 64-66
Future consequences, disregard for, 67, 70, 73
Goals, casework, 143-145
implementation of, 145-146
Good impression, 109, 110, 121
Good Impression Scale, 121
Guilt feelings, 9-10, 66-67,73, 120
Home environment, 116-118
Hostility, feelings of, 67, 73, 120
Identity diffusion, 25-27, 70
Identity formation, 111, 116-119, 149, 151
Illegitimacy:
incidence of (by age groups), 32-36
prevention of, 147-155
teen-age, 11

number of unwed mothers (1969), 11
as a social problem, 11-12
Intellectual efficiency, 102, 105, 107, 109
Interfaith marriages, 99-100
Interviews, with unmarried father, 47, 57, 59, 75-83
Inventories, psychological, 103-110
unwed fathers, 103-105
unwed mothers, 105-110
Involvement of unwed father:
in decision-making, 85-87, 90-96
effect on unwed mother, 90-96, 140
with social agency, 138, 139-143
Isolation, feelings of, 75
Jewish families, intermarriages, 99-100
Jewish Federation—Council of Greater Los Angeles, 17
Juvenile delinquents, 110
"Juvenile Unwed Father," 18
Legal rights, 11, 124
interest of parents in, 123, 124
Los Angeles County Department of Adoption, 18
Love relationships, 121, 137
Marital status, 38-39, 101
unmarried fathers, 41
unmarried mothers, 38-39, 40
Marriage as a solution, 1, 9-10, 82, 84, 92
Masculinity, search for, 118, 120, 149
Masturbation, 80-81
Maternity homes, 13
Maturity, 102, 103, 105, 108
Naming the father, 44-47
obtaining aid from unmarried mother, 46
National Council on Illegitimacy, 13
Natural Father Project, Los Angeles, 18
O.E.O. programs, 139
Parental relationships, 148-149, 150
need for improved, 150-151
Parents of unmarried couple, 27, 123-134
attitudes and values, 123-132
behavioral patterns, 123
child-rearing patterns, 123
church attendance, 129-130
concern for opinion of others, 132-134
conflict between, 129
criticism of self, 131-132
decision-making by, 127-128
disapproval of, 67
dominant member, 128, 149
family status, 125-126
happiness in marriage, 127
immigrant, 101-102
legal recourse, 123, 124
origins of, 101-102
reactions of, 7-9, 123-125
social agency support, 124
of teen-agers, 123-125
Permissiveness, 149, 151
Personal disjunctions, 110-113
measurement of, 111-113
Personality traits, 102-122
alienation, 114
attitude toward deviance, 114-116
home environment, 116-118
inventory scores, 103-110

personal disjunctions, 110-113
psychosocial profiles, 119-122
Personality inventory scores
unwed fathers, 103-105
unwed mothers, 105-110
Philadelphia Youth Center, 18
Pill, The, 11, 70
Planned Parenthood Association, 142
Poise, 102, 103, 108
Pregnancies:
incidence of, 43
previous, 101
Pregnancy, fear of, 67, 120
Pre-marital sex, views of parents, 67
Profiles, personality, 103
of unmarried fathers, 24, 119-122
of unmarried mothers, 25, 121-122
psychosocial, 119-122
Psychological tests, 27, 29, 153
Psychosocial profiles
unwed father, 119-122
unwed mother, 121-122
Prevention of illegitimacy, 147-155
factors affecting, 148-150
improved parental relationships, 148-149, 150-151
masculine/feminine identity, 149
suggestions of unwed parents, 150-152
Rape charges, 76
Reaching unmarried fathers, 17-19, 44-63, 138-139
approaches for, 54-59, 135-139
assertive, 55-56
motivational, 56, 58
attitude of social worker, 48
control group, 60
demonstration project, 17-19
interviewing father, 47, 57, 59
methods, 23-24
naming the father, 44-47
non-local unmarried fathers, 61, 62-63
obtaining aid from unmarried mother, 49-50, 51, 53
percentage seen and not seen, 61
projection of success in, 24
reasons for involving father, 48-49
success in reaching, 24, 50-51
Readers' Digest Almanac, 122
Recidivism, 42-43, 101, 152 154
Religious background, 98-100
of parents, 129-130
Report on the Jewish Population of Los Angeles, 122
Responsibilities of unmarried father, 76-77, 85
Responsibility, 102, 103, 105, 107-108, 110, 111
attitudes toward, 64
Role attainment, 117-118
Self-assurance, 102, 108
Self-control, 105, 107, 109, 110
Self-esteem, lack of, 111, 121, 149-150
Sex and the College Student, 155
Sex education, need for, 13, 138, 142-143, 154

Sexual act:
disregard for consequences, 70-73
exploitation and trickery, 70, 73
fear of pregnancy, 67, 120
female as aggressor, 67, 120
guilt feelings, 66, 73, 120
hostile feelings, 67, 73, 120
knowledge of contraceptives, 70-72
lack of consideration for partner, 67
lack of self-esteem, 70
meanings associated with, 68-69, 73
parental disapproval, 67
pregnancy "just happened," 70-71, 73
psychological aspects, 64-73
sexual ideology and, 64-73
stereotype views, 64
viewed as fun, 65-66, 73
Sexual identity, 118, 149
Sexual mores, 12
Sexual relations outside of marriage, 11-12
"Shotgun" weddings, 1
Social agencies, 10, 13-14
aid in decision-making, 85-87
approaches, 54-59
casework goals, 143-145, 153-154
involvement of unwed fathers with, 56, 138, 139-143
methods, 139-143, 153
motivational approaches, 56, 58
success in reaching father, 53
Social class background, 36-37, 98
Social maturity, 105, 107, 110, 111
Social relationships, 105, 107, 120
Social services, 16-17
Social workers, 66, 70
approaches used by, 135-139
areas for help, 137
assertive approach, 55-56
attitudes toward unmarried father, 48
basic premises, 135-138
casewok goals, 143-145
casework relationship, 21, 23, 29-30
clients' needs, 137, 142-143
getting name of father, 45-47
guidelines for, 144-145
involvement of unwed father with agency, 138, 139-143
reaching out to unwed father, 138-139
role of, 135-147
sex education, 142-143
Socialization, 102, 105, 107-110
Society:
attitude toward unmarried father, 1-2, 15-17
attitude toward unmarried mother, 1-2, 12-15
Standardized Case Recording Form, 25, 27, 28, 161 *ff.*
Standards for Services to Unmarried Parents, 17, 19
Sterilization, 12
Study Plan, 21-31

assumptions, 27-28
control groups, 22-24
data collection, 24-27
design of, 21-30
objectives, 21-24
psychological tests, 29
illegitimacy among, 11
unmarried fathers, 33-35
unmarried mothers, 32-35
Tolerance, 105, 107
Unmarried family, concept of, 13
Unmarried fathers:
definition, 22*n*
"From Shadow to Reality," 4-10, 75-83, 157-159
as participant, 15-17
Unmarried mothers:
as aggressor, 67, 120
aid in reaching the unmarried father, 49-50, 51, 53
definition, 22*n*
Unmarried parents:
adoptive status, 39, 42
age differentials, 35
background, 97-102
relationship between, 18
relationship with parents, 148-151
Venereal disease, 13
Vista Del Mar Child-Care Service, 17, 21, 23, 32, 44, 45, 49, 98, 100, 108, 109, 111
Welfare support of mother, 12